Let's Talk about Death

Let's Talk about Death

ASKING THE QUESTIONS THAT PROFOUNDLY CHANGE THE WAY WE LIVE AND DIE

STEVE GORDON

AND IRENE KACANDES

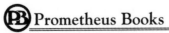
Prometheus Books

59 John Glenn Drive
Amherst, New York 14228

Published 2015 by Prometheus Books

Cover image © Mary Ellen McQuay / Media Bakery
Cover design by Jacqueline Nasso Cooke

Prometheus Books recognizes the following registered trademarks mentioned within the text: The Home Depot® and Hoyer®.

Inquiries should be addressed to
Prometheus Books
59 John Glenn Drive
Amherst, New York 14228
VOICE: 716–691–0133
FAX: 716–691–0137
WWW.PROMETHEUSBOOKS.COM

19 18 17 16 15   5 4 3 2 1

Library of Congress Cataloging-in-Publication Data

Gordon, Steve, 1956-
    Let's talk about death : asking the questions that profoundly change the way we live and die / by Steve Gordon and Irene Kacandes.
    pages cm
    Includes bibliographical references and index.
    ISBN 978-1-63388-112-9 (paperback) — ISBN 978-1-63388-113-6 (e-book)
    1. Death. 2. Grief. 3. Gordon, Steve, 1956—Correspondence. 4. Kacandes, Irene, 1958—Correspondence. I. Kacandes, Irene, 1958- II. Title.

HQ1073.G67 2015
306.9–dc23

                                                                          2015023526

Printed in the United States of America

To the hundreds of clients and family members who have allowed me to be a witness to their experiences with life, death, and mystery.

And to my wife, Nora, with thanks and love.

—Steve Gordon

For Lucie, Maria, Marie-Claude, Tina, Tom, Francesca, Elynor, Christine, Alfred, and all unacknowledged caretakers attending to the ill and dying.

—Irene Kacandes

CONTENTS

ACKNOWLEDGMENTS

Irene would like to express her gratitude to Michael Matt, Rebecca Rothfeld, and Er Li Peng for tracking down information; to Adam Z. Newton and Karlene Decosta for information about Jewish and Jamaican mourning customs, respectively; to Galina Rylkova and Marianne Kilani-Schoch for leads on things to read; to Bruce and Emily Duncan, Marianne Hirsch and Leo Spitzer, Agnès Rochat and Jean-Pierre Allamand, Becky Palmstrom, and to Father Deacon Gregory Uhrin and M. Lisa Uhrin, for listening to and sharing stories; to Dr. Kathryn Kirkland for allowing herself to be shadowed in the Palliative Care unit; to Deborah Canarella, Sheila Keenan, Steve Costello, Clancy Martin, Alexis Jetter, Jonathan Petropoulos, and Robert Donin for professional advice; to Jill Greenberg for seeing the potential in the book; and to Father Andrew Tregubov and the members of Holy Resurrection Orthodox Church of Claremont, New Hampshire, for listening to early drafts. Bernard Crettaz, Lucette Nobs, Isaac Ponte, and Barbara and Victor Ruffy helped me to understand Swiss attitudes toward mortality. Nora Pirquet and Jeffrey Title encouraged me throughout. I salute E. S. for his joie de vivre. Maria C. Kacandes-Kamil helped in so many different ways over such a long period of time that I cannot single out just one of them nor ever thank her enough. And Philippe Carrard almost always found a way to remind me to laugh. Finally, I want to acknowledge my brother-in-law, Steven Kamil, who believed that if telling his story could help others, he wanted it told.

Steve would like to thank the many family members, friends, and clients who were always willing to listen and to share their thoughts as

9

this book was developing, with particular thanks to his wife, Nora, and son, Jesse, for their unflagging support and faith.

Irene and Steve would like to thank Nancy Rosenfeld for her enthusiasm; Gail M. Patten for her meticulous preparation of the manuscript; Dean of the Faculty Michael Mastanduno and Dartmouth College for financial support; and Steven L. Mitchell and his whole team for their professionalism and helpful suggestions.

PREFACE

At the heart of this book is an unusual friendship that has its roots in murder and in a spring walk through a quiet neighborhood in a small New Hampshire town in the Upper Valley of the Connecticut River. That friendship developed through a long and frank dialogue between a college professor and a massage therapist, two average individuals, who chose to explore mortality together though neither was facing imminent death.

Irene Kacandes is a professor of comparative literature and German studies at Dartmouth College in Hanover, New Hampshire. In late January 2001, Irene, her friends, and quickly the whole community learned that Susanne and Half Zantop, also professors at the college, had been murdered in their home. The perpetrators had escaped without being seen, and a long, agonizing police investigation accompanied the stunned grieving of all who knew and loved the Zantops, including Irene. One of the more unexpected and certainly unpleasant aspects of getting through the ordeal involved contact with newspaper and television journalists who were focused on the crime and their theories about it and were distinctly uninterested in the wonderful lives the Zantops had led before becoming victims.

In early January 2002, as the one-year anniversary of the murders approached, Irene and other close friends of the Zantops decided to try to temper the inevitable renewed attention to the perpetrators—two local teenage thrill seekers who didn't even know the couple, it had turned out—and to instead commemorate their friends' *lives*. Irene and another friend volunteered to lead the effort and called Steve Gordon, the Sunday editor of the region's daily newspaper, the *Valley News*. He agreed to publish the friends' stories and photos of the Zantops in the form that Irene and her friend were proposing. For Irene, his kindness and cooperation contrasted starkly with the exploitative intrusiveness of other journalists whom the family and friends of the Zantops had had to deal with in the wake of the murders.

Years later, Irene read in that same local newspaper an article about that same Steve Gordon: he had made a midlife career switch and was working full-time as a massage therapist. He also had founded a nonprofit organization, The Hand to Heart Project, to give free massages to advanced cancer patients, including persons nearing death. Deeply impressed by both these actions, Irene sent off a donation to Hand to Heart. Although Steve did not consciously remember Irene when he saw her check, he felt compelled to call her house to thank her for the donation rather than just to send a note. Steve reached her husband and left a message, but he still didn't connect Irene with their previous interaction regarding the Zantops.

As professor of a course that covers, among other things, the local community, Irene thought that Steve could be a resource person, and she asked if he would be willing to be interviewed by two of her students about his nonprofit. He agreed, and even gave her feedback about the students and what a good job they had done with a difficult subject.

By way of thanks, Irene, who had not just experienced trauma through the violent loss of her friends, but had also written about it professionally, sent Steve a book and an article of hers that included accounts of how the Zantops' murders had transformed her approach to life. Steve, of course, then made the connection to their first contact over the Zantop commemoration and let Irene know of his desire to help trauma victims through massage. Learning of a workshop to be held at a local integrative-health group practice co-run by a former student who was also a trauma expert, Irene passed on the information to Steve; his participation in the workshop led him to join the group practice. Though that office is located close to the Dartmouth campus, Irene and Steve continued to remain in contact only through occasional e-mails.

By January 2011, Irene realized she was on the verge of being overwhelmed by her sadness about the ten-year anniversary of the murders of her friends and the situations of three family members facing their end of life. She shared some of her distress in an e-mail to Steve, who offered to lend her a set of CDs by the Buddhist teacher Joan Halifax called *Being with Dying*. For the second half of a long, cold winter, Halifax became Irene's companion as she drove around the Upper Valley, listening to the CDs in her car. As a practicing Eastern Orthodox Christian, Irene wasn't always in accord with the Buddhist philosophies and images that permeate *Being with Dying*, but Halifax's basic contention that we can use suffering as a way to connect with others and to cultivate compassion for all mortal beings profoundly moved her. She was also comforted by the idea that it was possible—as Halifax demonstrated—to speak about dying and death directly, extensively, peacefully, and with equanimity. In returning the CDs to Steve by mail, Irene suggested that they talk about them at some point.

When Steve and Irene finally met face-to-face on April 26, 2011, to take a walk and discuss *Being with Dying*, they had already known of each other for more than nine years. Maybe that was why the conversation flowed so easily, why one story after another came tumbling out. They paused to wonder if they were weird or morbid for spending two hours talking about death together the first time that they met. (They decided they were not.) After the walk, at a picnic table near Steve's office, they extended the conversation to the topic of writing about end-of-life issues. Steve was interested in passing on stories from the lives and deaths of people he had met through The Hand to Heart Project. Irene had been considering whether she needed to write more on trauma and sudden death. Back and forth their ideas went until one of them said: "Maybe it's a collaboration."

Wondering what such a collaboration would look like, they met a few more times in person in the weeks before Irene left for her parents' home in New York and then for Switzerland—a place where dying and death are more openly discussed in the press, in books, even in *Cafés mortels*, salons where the topic is death. During Irene's travels, the duo moved the conversation back to e-mail, beginning a long exchange of personal stories, ideas, and feelings related to mortality. By doing so without censoring or judging themselves or each other, they discovered that their views were shifting in unexpected and satisfying ways, even as they recognized disagreement on some topics, such as personal agency. They found the act of putting their thoughts into written words so helpful that, even when Irene returned from Europe, they continued to write to each other. In the end, convinced of the benefits of unfettered exchange, they decided that maybe they had the outline of a book that both needed to write. Back and forth the e-mails continued, with previously expressed thoughts regrouped around a series of questions. Rewriting while continuing to exchange new ideas, they noticed, was enhancing their understanding of their own views and each other's, as it also assisted each of them with emerging challenges in their personal lives related to relatives' and clients' continued decline or death.

When sharing their writing with a larger audience through publication became a reality, they decided to retain the original unfolding of their thoughts through e-mails exchanged over several years because it reflected not only their growing friendship but also the process they themselves had found so helpful to becoming more comfortable with discussing mortality: posing questions; offering answers; sharing things they'd read and daily experiences they were having; disagreeing with one another; and trying out a different idea by rewriting. Precisely because their growing understanding of mortality resulted from a writing process that unfolded in time—a time in which, naturally, other aspects of their lives were unfolding and influencing what they were writing—Steve Gordon and Irene Kacandes decided to retain the chronological presentation of the journey they've been on together, even as they also decided to modify, recast, and reorder some trains of thought so that they were more comprehensible to readers. Information or publications they came into contact with after the moment at which a specific e-mail was originally drafted were added to the notes. Similarly, as the purpose of what they were doing shifted from themselves trying to figure out mortality to trying to inspire others to have similar exchanges with their friends, they decided to organize helpful information for doing so into appendices.

The e-mails comprising *Let's Talk about Death* date from July 2011, shortly after the two met in person and just after Irene had been caring for her very ill father, to February 2015, when Irene and Steve were making final edits on their manuscript.

If the biggest obstacle to talking about mortality is getting a conversation going, then following how Irene and Steve have done just that could be helpful to others. They offer here the path of their joint meanderings because it embodies their shared conviction that when it comes to dealing with death, there are no right answers—certainly not answers that are right for everyone.

CHAPTER I

WHAT IS LIFE WITH DEATH?

La Tour-de-Peilz, Switzerland
4 July 2011

Dear Steve,

Thank you for your offer to exchange letters with me this summer while I am living and writing in the town where my husband, Philippe, grew up. It is a beautiful port on the shores of Lake Geneva in the French-speaking part of Switzerland. From my little writing desk in the living room I can see over the treetops, roofs, and lake to a few of the smaller mountains in the French Alps. (The biggest peaks usually can't be seen from this location.) Over the years that I've been coming here I have grown closer and closer to my husband's tiny, welcoming family, and I've made a few friends of my own through playing tennis and visiting the library at the Université de Lausanne, a short jaunt from here. Still, even with the joy of reconnecting with them and my husband, who has already been here for several weeks, I realize I am longing to be in dialogue with you. Is that because we've managed to bond over the topic of loss, and I am feeling the imminent loss of my father at this moment?

Since that day in late April when you and I met face-to-face and walked and talked, and the few follow-up chats we managed to fit into our busy schedules, I've finished up the academic year at Dartmouth, gotten our house in Lebanon, NH, ready for our absence and the arrival of tenants, traveled to White Plains, New York, where I grew up and where my parents still live, and I have just arrived here in Switzerland. Whew,

I am exhausted just writing that out, but even more exhausted from worrying about my father.

I believe I explained to you that my father has been in poor physical and mental health for some years now. He's not very old by today's standards, just eighty-one. But he's got diabetes, neuropathy, barely functioning kidneys, severely arthritic knees, and has already had a heart attack and open-heart surgery, all of which contribute to his limited mobility; some of those problems likely contribute to his increasingly severe dementia. We've been trying to take care of him at home. My mother does the greatest share of the caretaking, with part-time help from a home health aide. One of my sisters lives in New York City and makes the time to stop by often and check in on them, as does one of my brothers, who lives about an hour away. I go down from New Hampshire when I can take a break from my responsibilities at the university. (My other three siblings live thousands of miles away and have their own challenges to deal with right now.)

Dad had a terrible spring. He developed a urinary tract infection that was bad enough to send him to the hospital, where he then came down with new infections. He became so weak that he could no longer get in and out of bed, even with assistance, so eventually he entered a local rehabilitation home where he still is as I write you, and where the care, alas, has been inconsistent. Going back and forth to the hospital and acute-care facility and trying to deal with the healthcare system for more than a month has been exhausting for my mother and siblings. So it was an obvious choice to spend the time I had available between the end of the school year and departure for Europe being with my father and spelling my mother, sister, and brother from at least the daily grind of his care.

Seeing my father in so much pain, confusion, and distress was difficult, to be sure. When staff members who are patient and gentle were on duty, he remained calm, but when those who are generally in a rush were assigned to him, he would scream out in anticipation of the pain they were sure to cause him with a hurried and rough transfer from bed to wheelchair or wheelchair to toilet, from pajamas to clothes or vice versa. I would remind the staff to please tell him what was about to happen before they touched or moved him and to please stabilize his impossibly swollen and achy knees, but institutional protocol put me in the hallway more times than not, where I would shake from the sound of his screams and my own helplessness.

Once Dad was actually in the wheelchair or back in bed, I could be in charge. And that part felt easy, or at least very clear. My job was to try to comfort and engage him. Even when I had the sense that I wasn't succeeding at comforting or engaging him, I still felt the imperative to try over and over again. Patiently talking to him about anything and everything. Sitting in the corner of his room. Reading aloud little bits from the newspaper. Pushing him in his wheelchair outside. The June temperatures were generally warm but not yet scorching, and the place has a lovely garden and woods. I would point out to him the birds and rabbits near us and occasionally he would point one out to me. I would read him poetry. Rub his back. And often just sit in silence nearby.

Repeatedly I thought of you, Steve, and wondered how you actually do your work with the dying. I didn't wonder at all that you wanted to do it. Rather, I wondered about what kinds of massage you give to what kinds of patients. I wondered, too, how you know when to be active and when to quietly just be there, a silent witness to their suffering. A witness to their work of dying.

The other thing about these days spent with my father that I felt you would immediately understand was how easy it was for me to take an interest in the other residents in the facility. I tried to learn their names so that I could greet them when I passed them in the hall or outside. I smiled my widest smiles and shook hands with the stronger. I kissed several residents good-bye on my last visit and shed tears of recognition that I'd fallen in love with them and that chances were I would never see them again.

Why did all that come almost effortlessly? Where did that childhood disgust of the nursing homes we were made to visit as Girl Scouts disappear to? To put it another way, how did I get comfortable being with the elderly, the suffering, and the dying? I certainly never had a plan to become so. Knowing that I was there for just a few weeks definitely helped me to be as available to others as I could be. It helped me to engage with their pain and misery and to be on the lookout for joy and beauty so that I could share it with those around me. Could I have gotten up my energy and my optimism, though, if I'd already been doing this for months? If my engagement were open-ended? If I knew there was no break for me in sight?

Probably not, I suspect. Still, the reality of this visit for me was mainly peaceful. Dad is possibly going to die soon; a lot of these people might die soon; for all I know I could die soon. Those weren't happy thoughts, but they were acceptable thoughts. They were thoughts I accepted. So, now, in the immediate aftermath of this intense caretaking situation, of this immersion into an environment of pain, suffering, and imminent death, I find myself asking all kinds of questions related to our mortal end, especially as it is lived nowadays in North America.

How is it that people die so differently, of such different causes, and also with such seemingly different amounts and types of pain? How do so-called advances in medicine affect our dying? Why do so many of us seem to be dying protracted deaths? Perhaps most of all, my observations and engagements in that nursing home cause me to wonder about differences in attitudes toward pain, suffering, and mortality.

Some residents were so calm. Some seemed so depressed. A few, like my father, seemed agitated, if not downright terrified. And a few were perpetually cheerful. Maybe I'm on the wrong track here, but it seemed to me that those calmer and happier individuals must have had previous experiences that allowed them to accept, to truly take in, the idea that being alive means that they will feel pain, perhaps suffer, and for sure die one day. Maybe that knowledge of mortality and that attitude of acceptance have allowed them to live their lives—their "healthy" years and also perhaps their debilitated periods—in a more rich and conscious fashion.

What kinds of experiences do you suppose allow us to develop consciousness of death? What allows us to come to believe that dying is okay? Actually, more than that, that living with a consciousness of death is not just okay, it's actually beneficial to think some about our own dying. I don't endorse focusing exclusively on the fact that we will all die one day. Rather, I think I mean that having some kind of substrate knowledge of our mortality helps us to recognize life for what it is, temporary, and therefore to be treasured all the more deeply and consistently. Does it follow that I judge other people's choices—conscious or unconscious—about living with or refusing knowledge of death? I guess I'm writing to you now so that we can jointly puzzle out these issues.

The philosopher Friedrich Nietzsche is credited with saying that what doesn't kill you makes you stronger. Maybe that's part of the answer to why some people can come close to the dying, and even close to their own dying, and not be afraid or repulsed or numb. Speaking of Nietzsche, in the weeks I just spent with the very ill, I found myself recalling a lot of the literature I've read in my life yet had never before put into some category in my head called "lessons on mortality." I've been thinking, for instance, of a novel by the great German poet Rainer Maria Rilke. In an early chapter of *The Notebooks of Malte Laurids Brigge*, the protagonist recounts the death of one of his ancestors, his paternal grandfather. He reflects that each of us has our own death inside of us the way that a piece of fruit has its stone. Similar to the pits, seeds, and stones in various types of fruit, those deaths can be quite different. This death of his grandfather was very loud, protracted, and imposing; everyone in the castle was subjected to it, whether they wanted to be or not. His suffering filled every space.[1] Something about my father's struggle right now resembles what is described in those pages, or at least how they are stored in my memory.

Come to think of it, today is the anniversary of my own paternal grandfather's death. Which reminds me that I want to exchange thoughts with you at some point on the experience of sudden death, since my grandfather dropped dead of a massive heart attack at age sixty-five.

Do unexpected deaths like his, or like the murder of my friends the Zantops, or those caused by accidents come upon people so fast that there is no time for fear or other forms of anticipation? Do some of us die without knowing we are dying? Certainly popular belief holds this to be true. If consciousness is what distinguishes humans from other animals, can our consciousness fail us at the ultimate moment of our death?

I have to leave it here for now, Steve. I await your response to which I hope to "listen" attentively.

Irene

Cornish, NH
July 7, 2011

Good evening, Irene,

There is so much that is important, intriguing, and mystifying in your e-mail. I'll never cover everything it provoked in one reply.

First, about our connection: I think of it as a truly important new development in my life. Whatever comes of our exchange of thoughts and writings, I feel as though I'm opening an unexpected gift whose layers and true meaning I'm a long way from understanding.

Many of the questions you asked in your letter of July 4 may not be answerable. One of those, I suspect, is why you and I have come to be comfortable with the concept of death and being with people who are dying. I don't know much about your background—although since I have read your book *Daddy's War*,[2] I probably know more about yours than you do about mine—but I suspect that we had very different early-life experiences. If we are at the same point now in this regard, we arrived here by different routes. I know very well that I had a powerful fear of death for many years, and so I was confused to later discover my own comfort level with being around dying people. I wondered if it had something to do with the notion that if you stand really, really close to the monster, it won't see you. Or maybe just that if I'm in the room with death while it's tending to someone else, it won't notice me. Maybe I'm like Boo Radley from *To Kill a Mockingbird*, standing in the corner shadows.[3]

I attended a lot of wakes and funerals as a young person, but none of them, even those of older family members, had much of an impact on me. It was all pretty perfunctory, and talking about such things was not something we did in my family. I was an altar boy for several years and served at quite a few funerals and even more regular Masses, and the only significant difference between them that I recall now is the pervasive smell of incense at the former. And, of course, the casket.

Once, when I was quite young, my mother was in the hospital for some not-too-significant illness, and I made a card for her that said something like, "I hope you get better soon, but if not I've reserved a place in heaven for you." Can you imagine—suggesting she might die? I got some serious hell for that. Another time, when my grandfather was very sick following a car accident that damaged his heart, we all went to see him in the hospital, and when I went to his bedside, for some reason I spoke to him really loudly and slowly, as though being very ill meant he was probably deaf or simple-minded. I got in trouble for that, too. So, as you can see, I didn't have early exposures to illness and dying that fostered understanding or improved my level of comfort.

Why am I so at ease with it now? I wish I could say for sure. Maybe it's my underdog complex. When your formative years are spent feeling a little like an outsider within the family, you develop a keen sensitivity for the underdog. It doesn't seem a huge leap from there to being sensitive to anyone in difficult circumstances, including extreme illness. The trick, which I'm still learning, is to not stay in the feeling-bad-for place. What you asked about in your note—being a still and comforting presence for someone who is dying—isn't truly possible if what you feel is just pity. What people want is not pity but connection. If they want to talk, they want to talk honestly and even in some depth about what is happening and what will happen. When I can be clear that I'll do that with them, they often tell me things they haven't been able, or can't even try, to tell the people closest to them. And when they want silence, they usually make that known, if I'm open to noticing.

I've had few experiences more beautiful than sitting quietly with someone who is facing the end of his or her life. Having hands on the person in the act of massage, or simply compassionate touch, at the same time just adds to it for me. It's hard to explain, but the intimacy of it, the soul-to-soul contact that I sometimes feel by touching, takes the experience of mindfulness and presence to even greater depths. The massage that I provide through Hand to Heart depends on how clients are doing that day. If they are strong enough, which they often are, it looks much like a regular massage session on a table that I bring to their homes. If they aren't able to get on a table, even with my help, I might work with them on a sofa or on their bed. If they are close to death, it's different still, with me sitting or lying alongside them, my hands on them but moving slowly and lightly, if at all. Over time, it becomes less and less about the actual massage, and more and more about offering presence and compassion and the comfort of touch. I assume you knew all of this before your recent experiences with your father in the nursing home. You obviously know it now. I think of it as holding a space for someone to do or feel or process whatever is happening, without help or judgment from me.

When we took our first long walk in April, I believe I told you about a woman I'm working with who has severely advanced kidney disease. Her situation has taken up residency in my mind again lately. Consider this: She's not a great candidate for either dialysis or a transplant because of the type of disease she has. But she won't live all that much longer without some intervention, likely a transplant. Two family members have been eliminated as donors after tests showed they aren't good matches. That left one son, whom they hadn't been considering before. He has lived a life of somewhat-risky endeavors and has had many injuries, so they all thought it wasn't a good idea for him to have only one kidney.

Now they've discovered he's the only candidate. He says he'll do it, and he was cleared as a donor recently. But she's his mother, and she believes that while he's saying one thing, she might be hearing something different in the more subtle layers of his voice. Plus, even if they go through with it, there's a good chance her disease will destroy the donated kidney fairly soon, leaving her no better off and him with one kidney. How does she live with that prospect? Or that reality, if it comes to be? What she wants desperately is to be able to have a conversation with her husband and kids (the latter are in their forties) about all the nuances of the situation, all the ways of looking at it, including ways that might suggest the transplant isn't a good idea. However, she tells me that her husband is intensely focused on her getting healthy again, and so he cannot easily entertain any doubts about a transplant, not even her doubts. Her kids seem to be, at least outwardly, in the same place as their father.

There she is, facing the strong possibility of death—strong enough that she's done a lot of processing of what it would mean and how she might go about accepting it—and she is not sure how to get the people closest to her to hear what she's thinking. Because what she's thinking is that it might be better for her to accept dying of her disease now rather than accept her son's kidney. Our conversations during massage sessions have been frank and deep, almost as though we are both processing what is happening to her. I do feel pity, and I feel an embracing compassion that makes me want to keep the massage sessions going just so she can keep talking—so *we* can keep talking.

I'll also admit to being fascinated by her situation. She's not actually facing the end of her life right now, but she is carrying out this dance around the *concept* of death, and in a way, she's dancing alone, even in her crowded family ballroom. This is one form of life with death.

Maybe her situation preoccupies me because we are in a culture that avoids the topic. As you wrote, living with an acceptance and better understanding of death is better than not having those. Better for Life and better for Death, better for your experience of the actual moment of your death. When Mahatma Gandhi was assassinated, his first reaction to the bullet entering his body, or so I've read, was to quietly say, "Ram, Ram," an invoking of a Hindu deity. A prayer. I assume he did that so automatically because he knew, always, that death was inevitable, unpredictable, and as much a part of his life as his first and last breaths. He was ready.

I wonder, as you have, if even people meeting very sudden ends have that split second of awareness, and if being prepared makes that instant any easier.

When you ask me what kinds of experiences might lead people to consciousness of death as a part of life, I find myself thinking about suffering, illness, and loss as almost positive things, as the bringers of lessons throughout our lives. Are they lessons that could make us aware of all that we share with all other beings? This incomplete thought needs some time to sit in a warm place and rise.

Steve

FYI: I'm most of the way through *The Notebooks of Malte Laurids Brigge*. Interesting. I've been thinking I should go back through it with a highlighter. I keep coming on passages that speak to what I've been thinking about.

La Tour-de-Peilz
12 July 2011

Dear Steve,

Thanks for your thoughts of 7 July. I've tried to take in all you're sharing, and as hoped, it provoked many thoughts in me, in response and by association. Also, let me compliment you for tracking down and reading Rilke's *Malte Laurids Brigge*; I'm really impressed that you did that—and so quickly. It's usually only my very best students who follow up on references I make—not that I think of you as one of my students, mind you.

You say that if we're now in the same or at least a similar spot in relation to the dying, we got here by very different routes. That seems a certainty to me. To my mind, it's one of the great parts of being human: the variety of experience and yet the ability to relate and find similarities, too. You mentioned being at many wakes as a kid. You're right that I don't know a lot about you. Is there an Irish Catholic branch of your family? It interests me, because where I grew up in White Plains, New York, kids I knew, anyway, did not go to wakes or funerals. Though, now that I pause to think about it, we did have many Irish Catholic schoolmates. Maybe they just never mentioned the wakes. Be that as it may, when my mother, who had grown up in a small Greek-island village, took us, her four young daughters, to the wake of a neighbor, she was scolded for bad parenting: you don't bring children to a wake, she was told. For her it was second nature; death was part of life and you say good-bye to people who have died.

Our mother used to tell us many stories about her village childhood, including how everybody would keep the elderly and the ill company—at home, of course. And when those folks died, everybody would continue to keep them—there doesn't seem to have been such a sharp line between the ill person and the dead person—company for a while, and then there would be a funeral and they'd be buried. When the flesh had broken down, the bones would be dug up to make room in the cemetery for the next person, and the bones would be put in a box and the box in the cemetery's bone house. Our favorite story was of when they dug someone up once and realized it was too soon. So they simply reinterred him. I don't remember being disgusted by that story, just surprised. I don't think disgust was an emotion our mother ever expressed around the topic of death, nor fear. It was a long time before I saw the ossuary in our mother's village for myself. By then, I was already full of longing for times and places where dying and death were an acknowledged part of the life cycle. There must be so many benefits to growing up with that attitude.

Not all of my early experiences with death were peaceful, though. I mentioned my paternal grandfather's sudden end in my last letter, because it was the anniversary of his death, the Fourth of July. I was twelve; he was sixty-five. We were actually spending the holiday with my mother's side of the family. When the paternal relatives in Jersey tracked us down by telephone to my Uncle Alex in Upstate New York, my father threw us kids in the car immediately. We knew something was really wrong when he yelled at us because we started singing, something we did a lot in those days to comfort and entertain ourselves, and something that our father usually enjoyed, even bragged about to others. The car ride seemed endless. The next thing I recall clearly is the funeral itself, which was a traditional Greek Orthodox service with an open casket. My grandmother kept screaming to my grandfather to open his eyes. I don't remember how good my Greek was at the time, so I can't be sure I was following everything she said. Still, I do feel certain that everyone in that church was feeling her pain; I know I was—viscerally. I recounted my thoughts around my father's reaction to his father's death in my book *Daddy's War*. You might remember that my father was full of regret for never having resolved feelings of resentment about his father's behavior when the family was separated during the Second World War. Suddenly it was too late and there was no chance to straighten it out, put the relationship on another footing, or tell his father that he loved him. My father was miserable.[4] The main point here would be that I, too, got a lot of mixed messages about death when I was younger.

Speaking of past experiences, I like your underdog theory—that perhaps you find it so easy to be compassionate with individuals in pain, physical and mental, because you yourself have known suffering. I have some evidence for your hypothesis from my own family. I've told you a bit about my father's current situation and have alluded to two other relatives who have been ill for years and are probably close to the end of their lives. One is my Swiss mother-in-law, Mireille, who'd lived an extremely healthy and independent life into her early nineties and then had a stroke. She recovered most of her speech and some use of her right side, but not enough to live alone. She's still alive at ninety-six and is being taken care of in her own apartment by my husband's sisters. The other individual is my brother-in-law. Steve is married to my oldest sister,

Maria, and they live in London with their two teenage daughters. Steve was diagnosed eleven years ago with a rare disease called a chordoma. Ever heard of it? It is a tumor that forms at the skull base or in the spine of the fetus in utero. At some point in the person's life, the tumor starts to grow, or grow more quickly and, depending on its location, leads to death sooner or later. Maria has been indefatigable in searching out treatments, and Steve has been fiercely determined to survive. So, he, too, is still alive, though now very weak and with limited mobility, some seven surgeries and a dozen experimental treatments later.

The evidence for your underdog thesis is that my ill family members have been able to demonstrate a lot of compassion for each other: my mother-in-law for Steve and my father; Steve for my mother-in-law and my father; my father, until recently due to his increasing dementia, for Steve and Mireille, about both of whom he would frequently ask. Mireille doesn't write to anybody anymore, but she has written to Steve. I'm not sure how much writing Steve does these days, but recently he's written to Mireille. I can't say, alas, that these ill folks have always had the same concern for their caretakers who have been sacrificing their lives to do the caretaking in all three cases for years now. Still, I count it as a good thing that our family invalids have sometimes been able to express concern for one another, and I believe that's mainly because they feel they can identify with aspects of the others' plights. I guess the next logical question would be, then, how do we learn to extend our compassion to many others, including those with whom we do not share as much? Or maybe the talent is to recognize our plight in all other humans. Death is certainly one element all humanity shares, actually all sentient beings share, no?

Speaking of sharing, before I run out of energy I want to thank you for telling me about your client with kidney disease. Even though I am mercifully not ill myself at the moment, I have been witness to too many family scenes where the most urgent issue doesn't seem to get discussed or, to take up one of your metaphors, where everyone seems to be dancing around the issue without engaging it directly. Rather than focus on the personal here, I'd like to suggest a connection between what you've written me about that family and something that's been bugging me about our society at large: when it comes to decisions about end-of-life care, we Americans really don't have many options for thorough discussion. I know, I know. Some hospitals, including our own Dartmouth-Hitchcock Medical Center, have instituted "shared decision making" that supposedly brings the patient and the patient's wishes more integrally into the conversation about what should happen next. And many hospitals now have palliative care units where highly trained staff members are familiar with the latest options for pain treatment and end-of-life care. Still, it seems to me that these are not universally available and, in any case, they are only small pieces of a very complicated puzzle that concerns not just the patient and not just the hospital.

We seem to have no forum that allows us to think outside a medico-technological framework that is completely oriented to healing disease. Don't get me wrong: I'm on board with healing. But I'm not subscribing to seemingly endless treatment when healing is not really possible. We can't "heal" the reality of mortality. You've probably seen the same statistics I have about the huge percentage of any individual American's expenditures for healthcare being spent during the last months of life. Shouldn't we all pause to think about that for a minute, or for more than a minute? Isn't it perverse to think of death as failure, as something that medicine can or at least should be able to fix?

That's why I got so angry about the "death panel" debacle. I'm sure you recall how quickly and widely Sarah Palin's phrase got picked up after she first used it as a tool against healthcare reform in August 2009 by writing:

> The America I know and love is not one in which my parents or my baby with Downs Syndrome will have to stand in front of Obama's "death panel" so his bureaucrats can decide, based on a subjective judgment of their "level of productivity in society," whether they are worthy of health care. Such a system is downright evil.[5]

To my mind, even though Palin appears to have been aiming at shutting down healthcare reform, in the long term, the even more destructive result of the bogeyman Palin created is that it shut down a golden opportunity for us as a society to think through the consequences of medicine and technology reigning supreme and unquestioned as the answer to everything. As the situation of your client with kidney disease makes clear, there are so many dimensions to facing severe illness. Just because transplants are possible and just because a donor exists may not mean that a transplant is automatically the best next step. How I long to participate in discussions where the consequences, shorter and longer term, of medical interventions could be aired with the help of many specialists who will bring a relevant perspective, doctors of many types, yes, but also psychologists, spiritual advisors, and to my mind, even financial ones.

To bring it closer to home—to my home—my mother-in-law now has a pacemaker. If it successfully restarts her heart whenever it falters, how does her inevitable death actually happen? She's getting weaker and weaker. Will everything in her body be ready to die and yet her heart will keep ticking? What will that feel like for her? At age ninety-six, she experiences fewer and fewer days where she feels truly well. Am I evil for wondering whether that pacemaker was a good idea?[6]

I have this particularly on my mind because the facility where my father is currently staying tried to force us to authorize a pacemaker for him. His blood pressure and pulse are generally very low, and they have some protocol that says that if a patient's heart rate falls below forty beats per minute—I believe that's the figure they cited—the patient must be sent to the hospital. They've already bounced my father to the hospital twice solely for this reason, and since there's really nothing they can do for him there, he gets sent back to the nursing home. The trips jostle his already-painful joints, and any change of location severely disorients him. At the nursing home's insistence that he would not be able to stay there unless he got a pacemaker, we ended up scheduling a visit for him with a leading pacemaker specialist in Manhattan. Thank the Lord the doctor agreed with us that the device was not going to improve Dad's quality of life. So what, please tell me, would be the justification for inflicting that procedure on him at this time? He was feeling worse than ever for a full week in the wake of being transported between the care facility in Westchester and the specialist's office in Manhattan. As far as I could tell, we inflicted that pain on my father because we can't handle his care in our home and producing the response from the specialist was the only way the nursing home would let him stay there. Isn't there something wrong with this picture?

All these events make me feel desperate to puzzle out these issues about illness, medical interventions, dying, and death. At the same time, I am eager to focus on life and how lucky I feel to be together with the man I love. I don't see the two efforts as mutually exclusive. The life force in me is very strong right now. Though I'm not sure I'm expressing this thought just right, I feel the desire to live and to live well is bolstered by me being able to take in and know a bit about the dying, the suffering, and the lurking deaths—including my own eventual death—that surround me.

Okay, I can see that my literary training is inevitably and I hope helpfully going to come into our exchange again. The scene that comes to my mind now is from Thomas Mann's masterpiece *The Magic Mountain*. (Warning, this one is really long!) In it, the protagonist, one Hans Castorp, goes to visit his cousin in a sanatorium in Davos, Switzerland. (I promise I did not plan for this to come together so poetically.) It's a simplification, but I think true to say that Castorp falls in love with sickness; in any case, he himself becomes a patient on the Magic Mountain. At one point he goes for a walk, gets lost in a snowstorm, blacks out or falls asleep—it's not completely clear which—and almost dies. He has a very complicated vision and comes back to consciousness with the thought that he must give death no sovereignty over him.[7] I have alternately loved and hated this novel for all kinds of reasons, yet that revelation has always seemed completely correct to me. Knowledge that death is there, yes, but not surrendering life to death in the sense of forgetting to do all the living we are capable of doing at all times, including the special kind of living that happens when one is ill or as one is dying. Do you see what I mean? I feel like I can only repeat for now, how important it feels to me to learn to express this thought as effectively as possible. Maybe that's another goal in my writing to you? To not let my own concerns about these dilemmas be shut down the way the specter of "death panels" shut down national debate on discussing with informed health-care providers critical decisions.

So, to bring it back closer to something you wrote in your last missive to me: yes, yes, yes: life *with* death. That makes perfect sense to me. There are so many more thoughts your letter triggered, but I guess I'll stop here for now and await your reactions.

Irene

Cornish, NH
July 20, 2011

Dear Irene,

Great. Now I have to read *The Magic Mountain*. And I know it's going to take a lot longer than reading *Malte Laurids Brigge*. I did enjoy that short novel, though. Many passages from it keep coming back to me, including this observation by the narrator early on, which rings true as I spend all this time contemplating, reading, and writing about dying and death: "I am learning to see. Why, I cannot say, but all things enter more deeply into me; nor do the impressions remain at the level where they used to cease. There is a place within me of which I knew nothing. Now all things tend that way. I do not know what happens there."[8]

I love the mystery in that thought, the recognition that great and important things are happening inside, even if Herr Brigge doesn't understand them. I've come to realize that the greatest and most important things that happen to us all happen inside, and that it is not necessary to understand them.

There is no greater mystery in life than death. No one knows what it will be like, not even the strongest believer in any of the many religious traditions that spell out their notions of death and an afterlife. Belief can be powerful, even powerful enough to feel like certainty, but it cannot be the same as knowledge. That is the nature of faith, I suppose. And knowledge of exactly what happens at the moment of death and the moment right after eludes us all. That must be among the reasons it is both so fascinating and so frightening to so many of us. It must also be why so many people cling so powerfully to life. If we knew for certain what comes after this life, we might let go of life a little more easily, even when it means losing what we have come to love.

But we don't. We "battle," "fight," and "struggle against" disease and decline. If we are to believe what we read in obituaries, the last days and months of life are often defined by struggle and fight: "*So-and-so* died after a courageous battle with cancer." We spoke briefly during our April walk about being uncomfortable with this militaristic language, this focus on winning and losing. To me it sometimes seems shallow and misguided, like the loss of an opportunity to engage in a positive, fruitful way with suffering and loss. The late writer and philosopher John O'Donohue made that the point of a wonderful blessing he wrote in his last book, *To Bless the Space between Us* (published posthumously, by the way, not long after he died of a heart attack in his early fifties). "Now is the time of dark invitation," he writes at the start of "For a Friend on the Arrival of Illness."[9] In the next several lines, he spells out beautifully what it must feel like to have your life taken over by life-threatening disease. "You feel that against your will a stranger has married your heart."

And then he turns from such despair and invites the reader to look at his or her misfortune straight on, to ask it why it has come, to learn from it, to find healing where none seemed possible.

May you find in yourself
A courageous hospitality
Towards what is difficult,
Painful and unknown.[10]

It seems such a civilized, peaceful way to approach illness and dying. But as much as I love O'Donohue's message, and in particular his wonderful phrase "courageous hospitality," I wonder if it might underestimate the need that people have to control what is happening to them and to resist giving in, even to an incurable disease like the one your brother-in-law has.

I have a middle-aged client who has been in treatment for colon cancer for about four years. She's a psychoanalyst, and she has spent a lot of time thinking about her prospects and about how she is handling everything that is happening to her. I mentioned to her recently that I was mulling over the idea that it would be nice to replace the combat rhetoric people employ when speaking about cancer and other diseases with something less aggressive. She was kind enough not to tell me I was wrong, instead saying she wanted to write something and send it to me. She did. Her essay started by saying that she, too, used to have little patience for all the "battling" going on in hospital rooms and in the homes of the very ill. She continued:

> Now I have cancer and have had chemotherapy for most of the past four years. Things have changed. Getting through this has felt like a long, miserable, arduous, continuous series of battles. It has been a goddam war to stay alive. I had to fight to wake up and force myself to go to the hospital. I had to fight my urges to disconnect myself from tubes and run away. I had to fight my fear, sadness and panic around the smiling nurses and doctors. . . . During one treatment, a patient screamed for hours. It was a harrowing sound. It sounded like she was being tortured. In any other situation, I could walk away, but I was captive. I assumed she was mentally unbalanced, but then I realized she was doing what I felt like doing. Maybe she was just more honest. . . .

I have heard people talk about accepting and embracing cancer. Acceptance is important. If you deny its existence, it will definitely kill you. I have accepted it as the enemy. I must be stronger than it. I cannot love it. I will not accept that it will determine my fate. . . . I am a warrior for life, and it is how I stay alive.[11]

Reading her words is like getting a strong dose of reality to challenge my fuzzy notions about taking a softer approach to life-threatening disease. I still believe it might make the experience of illness and of approaching death less anxiety-filled if one accepts that death, whenever it comes, is as much a part of nature as everything that comes before it. It can't be wrong, though, to resist the end, to work mightily to stay alive. To, as you say, accept death and live life fully at the same time. Up to a point. Where that point is, exactly, is part of the mystery. Still, if what comes before it is best characterized by some people as a battle, who am I to question? Perhaps that illusion of control is powerful enough to keep people alive. Not forever, of course.

One of my favorite massage-therapy clients is an eighty-seven-year-old woman who has numerous health issues but is still strong, mentally and physically, and still going out most weeks for exercise, movies with a daughter, and regular meetings of a local religious group. We have had some wonderful conversations over the years, about her life and mine, her experiences as a recovering alcoholic, family issues, and, of course, death. She once told me that she is very much afraid of dying. And then she rethought: "No, that's not right. I'm not afraid of dying. I'm afraid of being dead." Then she laughed and added: "Which, when you think about it, is the ultimate control issue!"

And with that . . .

Steve

La Tour
27 July 2011

Dear Steve,

The chance to talk out these difficult subjects with you has been so helpful that I feel like I can only repeat, thank you for sharing. And speaking of sharing, just a brief note today to let you know that Mom succeeded in snatching Dad out of the healthcare system, or rather, at least out of its institutions. The nursing home was a nightmare, as you've probably gathered from my previous missives. Fundamentally, the staff there just didn't seem interested enough in taking care of him. They bounced him yet again to the hospital since I last wrote you. And with the help of an insightful social worker at the hospital who seemed to register how destructive this yo-yoing was for Dad, Mom was able to get his release to home authorized. I gather you need such authorization if you're going to receive Medicare benefits for home care. In other words, evidently his release involved our family giving guarantees of hiring more help, since Dad still can't move himself or assist with moves, and since (due to his heavy weight) he's considered to need two helpers for any transfer. Hence, our dining room has been dismantled and set up as a bedroom for a night nurse. A hospital bed was delivered for Dad. Mom's worried about how we'll pay for it all—Medicare pays for some things, but not for lots of other things that Dad requires at this stage. Mom's also anxious about having to share her home, especially at night, with a stranger, but she's so relieved to have Dad home, she's putting those concerns on hold for now. Our dining room was such an important place for family gatherings; it's hard for me not to feel, even from so far away, some sadness over its disappearance. More urgently, I'm terribly worried about whether Mom can accept the help she'll need to manage Dad at home. And yet, with all that on my mind, I mostly feel great relief and gratitude for Dad being out of uninterested and hurried hands.

i.

CHAPTER 2

IS DYING AN INJUSTICE?

Cornish, NH
August 21, 2011

Dear Irene,

I've been visiting over the last several months with a wonderful woman in Vermont as part of The Hand to Heart Project. I have been to see this particular person many times, and from the very first of our conversations, she was clear that she knew her ovarian cancer would end her life at some point. She is not quite fifty years old, married, has no children, owns her own business, and dotes on her golden retriever as much as she does her husband.

She has been in treatment for cancer for more than three years and recently went through the difficult, mind-boggling, spiritual transition from working toward a medical reprieve into knowing that that is impossible. Now, she is focused on how she wants to live with cancer before she dies of it. Because she isn't getting out much, that change is taking place largely in her closest relationships, and mostly with people who don't want her to—as they see it—give up.

Beth is a cheerful, affectionate person by nature. Bright, wide-set eyes, prematurely gray hair, and a smile as broad as her face all make for a warm, open demeanor that you might expect of an old friend. She told her husband when she was diagnosed that she would do the best she could to get rid of the disease, but it would have to be done her way. If that had to involve surgery and chemotherapy, then so be it. But the primary force would be laughter. Mostly, she has held to that, from what I have seen. Certainly we have laughed a lot during my visits—about her family; her dog, Brinkley; her illness; and the longtime customers of her hair salon, whom she misses dearly. In some moments, the pain and the inexorable nature of her decline become a heavier weight than she can bear, and she struggles to smile when I arrive. On those days we talk.

Among the memories she has shared is one dealing with what it was like to grow up with a mother who had multiple sclerosis and was in a wheelchair for many years. That's why Beth and her husband decided not to have children: She didn't want to risk developing that disease while they were young, or perhaps passing it on to them.[1] She has two sisters whom she loves, although she's told me that they can be protective to a point bordering on controlling. One of them was visiting with her the first time I went, and she made a point of leaving us alone and heading down to the basement. It was much later that I learned that she'd actually just stayed on the stairs, out of sight but within hearing distance, to make sure Beth was safe. Much later, her other sister was instructing her on what would happen next whether Beth liked the idea or not, and Beth brought her up short with: "Now wait a minute. Which one of us is dying here?"

Her spirits were quite low when I arrived one recent morning. She had become too weak to get onto the massage table, so we were doing the sessions with her on a sofa, and that's where she was when I arrived. I pulled up a chair to talk for a while first, and she told me that the delivery of a wheelchair and other medical equipment had brought her mother to mind in ways that made the advance of her own disease very concrete— and depressing.

I asked her what it was about dying that bothered her the most. She took very little time to think about it, and replied, "It's just being pulled out of this life so suddenly, with no say in it."

It wasn't right. It seemed an injustice.

Her answer has stayed with me because of the sharp focus it brought to one of the most important questions I hear people raise about death—

especially the deaths of people who are not elderly. Is death unfair? Is it unjust that a child can die of a disease, a young man or woman die in a war, a middle-aged spouse or parent succumb to cancer or a heart attack? That anyone at any age can meet their death in an auto accident, a plane crash, or a violent crime?

The answer, I think, is no. But it's simplistic to say only that. To my mind, there are at least two ways to divide the question, and the answer might be different for each. Is death an injustice to the person who is dying or has died? And is death an injustice to those left behind?

Answering either has to begin with me understanding that there is nothing about being born that guarantees a long life. On average, a child born today in North America has a life expectancy of nearly eighty years, about double the figure from only several generations ago. But no baby is assured of reaching that age, or anything beyond it. That number accounts for people who died during their first year of life, in their twenties, in their fifties, and even in their nineties. Life is tenuous; it can end for myriad reasons at any one of those ages and any age in between. If that is so, how can it be unjust to die "young"? It is neither just nor unjust. It's simply life as a mortal.

If we embrace that truth, we might find it easier to face the end of life whenever it comes; but more important, we might find it easier, even necessary, to live each day and each year in a way that treasures life precisely for its ephemeral nature.

But what if you are not the one who is dying? What if you are a child losing a father, a mother losing a child, a young woman losing a husband? Isn't that unjust?

Again, I would say no. There is a difference between painful and unjustly painful. That difference might seem like semantics to some, but you will understand, as a professor of literature, the importance of subtleties in the exact words we choose. Pain is unpleasant, but if it is also unfairly imposed, then we can see ourselves as victims, either of fate or of whomever we find to blame. Being a victim is rarely constructive and leaves little room for growth. If pain is just pain—an unpleasant part of life, but one we share with all other beings—then we aren't victims. We're just people in pain, and pain is no more permanent than bliss—or life.

You know that I have a wife, a son, a daughter-in-law, and two wonderful granddaughters. They are all important to me, and losing any of them would be an immeasurable loss. Still, odd as this exercise might sound, I have envisioned the deaths of each one of them. Not the act of dying, but the loss itself. I try to imagine how I would feel if some event stole one or more of them away. How would I carry on? What would it mean to lose someone whose life I hold dear?

It would be painful beyond words. But it would not be something done *to* me. I would not be a victim of that person's death. In the end, I would hope to see myself as a beneficiary of his or her life, however long or short it was. And I would move on in my own life to the next part, the part that includes that person as a vivid, colorful, treasured memory, just as I assume they would move into the next phases of their lives if I were the one to die, which, after all, is at least as likely.

Does this make sense?

S.

La Tour-de-Peilz
22 August 2011

Dear Steve,

Thanks for picking up the ball again; I hadn't realized how much time had passed since my last note. August always goes by fast here because we have my sister-in-law's birthday—out of which we make a family party that's a little like Christmas in August—and because I'm usually getting ready to go teach, either at the college in New Hampshire or at our program abroad in Berlin. This year it'll be Berlin.

I think you know how much I appreciate being able to exchange thoughts with you on these subjects that so few people seem comfortable addressing directly; I'll try not to say thank you all the time, and yet . . . today I also want to express my gratitude to you for sharing with me specifically about Beth. It sounds like she is quite a remarkable woman! I appreciate and admire the clarity of sentiment and the aptness of the metaphor reflected by her remark to you about being pulled out of her life. I'm sorry to hear that she is indeed close to the end of her time on Earth.

So now to your question to me: Does what you're writing about death being simply a part of life and therefore as neither just nor unjust make sense to me? Well, most of it does. I definitely think that it is bizarre when people remark, as Woody Allen supposedly has, that they are okay with death, they just don't want it to happen to them. I actually had a friend say something similar to me once, and I was so surprised that a mature adult could hold this belief that I could only laugh awkwardly in reply.

After all, would you really want to be alive if all your friends and family had died? The places you'd be in might be the same, but the human landscape would be unfamiliar. Sure, you could potentially make new friends, but they wouldn't have a shared history with you, the kind that binds us into networks, the kind that makes us feel known.

Then there's the idea you bring up of pain, loss, and death as dimensions of life that we share with other sentient beings. To wish we had a fate different from others is to separate ourselves from others. Wouldn't it be disconcerting to *not* experience precisely what every person you've ever known was going to experience or already had experienced? In this point, however, also lies the rub for me, because while it's true that we will each die, that we all have that in common, it's also true that human beings die very different deaths. We die at younger or older ages, and from very different causes that at least from this side of life appear to involve very different amounts of pain. Of course you know that, and you've written it in your letter. Still, I can't put into the same group the child who is killed by a sniper's bullet and the fifty-year-old who succumbs to cancer.

To get at this issue another way, earlier this summer I read the last book by David Servan-Schreiber, a French psychiatrist who worked mainly in the United States and is best known for an "anti-cancer" method of eating and exercising that he published and gave lectures on worldwide. Well, he himself was diagnosed with brain cancer in his thirties, had a metastasis in 2010, and died in July of this year. The book I read was the last he completed, and it narrates his relapse, his final treatments, and his recognition that he is going to die. There are lots of things to admire in Servan-Schreiber and in how he writes about his life and his work. What stood out for me the most, I think, is precisely what he writes on this subject of "justice." When it's clear that the treatments are not helping him to go into remission, he reports, "I remind myself of the evidence that, after all, I'm not the only one who has to die."[2] This thought made me laugh, and its perspective sits better with me than one that expresses a wish to escape death. He continues:

> It's not as if someone is unjustly punishing me, throwing me into the dungeon with water and dry bread. No, everybody must pass this way one day. That my turn is arriving earlier is sad, but it's not a monstrous injustice. I've been fortunate to have had extraordinary encounters, to have known love, to have had children, to have had brothers and amazing friends, to have left my mark. I've lived through rich experiences, cancer included. I don't have the sense of having frittered away my life.[3]

I like the way Servan-Schreiber makes central to his thinking that death is a part of all life and that all humans will go that way. Just as much, I appreciate that he is able to take in that he himself has done a huge amount of living.

I remember distinctly a moment in my own past—it was sometime after I got situated in my current job at Dartmouth—when I truly registered the bounty of blessings I'd been the recipient of: I've been able to get a fabulous education, learn languages, travel, connect with people in many parts of the world, find happiness in my intimate relationships, enjoy a huge family and circle of friends. So, my thinking has gone since then, if I do die tomorrow by accident, or sometime soon due to an illness, it certainly won't be a tragedy, to my mind, not even if I meet a violent death. I wouldn't want to be remembered for that means of death. Rather, I would want it to be remembered that while I had the chance, I tried to live my life as fully as I could. I've thought about putting a note with my last will and testament that reminds my friends of this, and specifically that that's how I see it—well, at that point, I guess it'll be "saw it"—myself. I can't dictate that those who knew me should not be sad, of course, but I really do wonder if it's not a good thing to leave behind a message that says, "I'm okay with this life ending. It's been really great while it lasted." And like Servan-Schreiber with his cancer, I count even my greatest sorrows and losses as part of this rich and rewarding life lived.

Believe me, I do get the sadness part. I have lost so many people whom I have loved, and I am often sad as I miss them in my life. I'm not volunteering to go tomorrow if I don't have to. So I get, too, what Beth told you about being pulled out of her life. I think her honesty on that score is what makes her so compelling to me. She loves life and doesn't want to leave it just yet.

That train of thought seems like a logical whole and yet even as I type those words, a question pushes itself into my consciousness: what about children or the poor or civilian populations in so many places in the world (including in our own country, of course) who do not have a genuine chance at growing up with even a modicum of health or peace, through no fault of their own? Can we really say that their deaths, as a result of the circumstances, are fair? It is a part of life on Earth as we know it, to be sure. But *fair*? I don't think so.

I couldn't agree more with what you've said about the negative effects of self-pity and adopting victimhood. I've read a great article on this topic called "Surviving Victim Talk," by legal scholar Martha Minow.[4] What I've taken most to heart from her argument is that whom we consider to be victims says a lot about who we are as a society. I wonder if where I end up on this matter is not so much saying that there are no unjust deaths, as much as saying that most of our deaths will *not* be tragic. I find myself wanting to urge people I know to exercise great caution about whose death we label in that way. Simultaneously, we should be working to do something to improve the conditions of life so many must endure that lead to deaths we should consider unjust and a shameful reflection on ourselves and our priorities.

Now I find myself wanting to ask you: does that make sense?

i.

Cornish, NH

September 12, 2011

Dear Irene,

Odd that you have focused so much on the deaths of children. Odd, because while I don't think I'm changing my mind about whether such deaths are fair or unfair, just or unjust, I also know they provide a powerful and emotional challenge to my way of thinking.

Last spring, the *New Yorker* magazine had a piece by Aleksandar Hemon recounting in heartbreaking detail the death of his very young daughter, who had a rare brain cancer.[5] The progress of the disease brought one setback after another, and the parents watched their little girl suffer each step of the way. They suffered each setback and each spasm of pain with her, until the moment when they told one of the doctors to stop applying chest compressions and accepted that she was gone. Difficult as it was to read the stark details of the father's account, I found I was most troubled by one statement he made near the end of the article:

> One of the most despicable religious fallacies is that suffering is ennobling—that it is a step on the path to some kind of enlightenment or salvation. Isabel's suffering and death did nothing for her, or us, or the world. We learned no lessons worth learning; we acquired no experience that could benefit anyone. Isabel most certainly did not earn

ascension to a better place, as there was no better place for her than at home with her family. Without Isabel, Teri and I were left with oceans of love we could no longer dispense; we found ourselves with an excess of time that we used to devote to her; we had to live in a void that could be filled only by Isabel. Her indelible absence is now an organ in our bodies, whose sole function is a continuous secretion of sorrow.[6]

What a powerful statement of grief. I don't accept the truth of it, though. While I was not surprised, I was saddened that someone who had gone through the trauma he and his wife had endured would come out of it with such pain and anger. Those feelings would make sense for a time after the child's death, yet I wished—for him and for those reading the magazine—that in the time it took to write and edit his article, those hard edges could have softened, or that he had waited until they had before writing. Maybe the writing itself was an exercise in that direction.

I think it is an important truth, in fact, that suffering *is* ennobling, if by "ennobling" we mean bringing us some measure of enlightenment, some clearer idea of our purpose on Earth, some greater and deeper connection with other beings. I believe that that author likely will think, and maybe act, differently if he sees another child suffering, or other parents living something like his nightmare. It seems likely that he developed meaningful connections with doctors or nurses caring for his daughter, connections he would never have made otherwise and that will inform some aspects of his life from that point on. The rest of his life is built on the foundation of that loss, and if there is nothing but pain and anger, then the loss is, sadly, multiplied.

I think the issue might be that the original question we posed regarding death as just or unjust presents a false choice. It is neither—and perhaps both. A young child dying of a disease cannot appreciate the philosophical or spiritual nuances at play when considering human mortality. She experiences what comes her way with an equanimity that many adults see as a lesson in courage, when it is in fact a product of innocence. That the death of such a child would seem unfair is natural to those watching it, but in fact it fits as perfectly into the spectrum of human life as any other death. It is neither just nor unjust, and it is exquisitely painful to watch.

Whether it is fair, unfair, or neither plays no role in how painful such a death is in the short term. I wonder, though, if realizing or accepting that death is not a matter of justice can help survivors in the longer term, once their grief is less sharp.

Back to my client Beth for a moment. She had clung pretty fiercely, early on, to the idea that she might be able to use the power of her spirit and the support of her loved ones—and the assistance of modern medicine—to rid herself of cancer. Of course, she also always knew that healing wasn't guaranteed, and by the time I met her, she had accepted that her prospects were not good. She was still getting chemotherapy, but she did not expect a cure, only the possibility of more time with her husband, her dog, and other loved ones. In spite of her comment to me that day about being pulled unfairly from her life, I have more often seen that she knows she will die of cancer and accepts that she has no basis on which to declare that it shouldn't be happening to her.

She has embraced her mortality in all its inevitability. For the most part, her husband has, as well, although as often happens, he wants her to continue pushing forward with treatments that might, just might, lead to a miracle. Her sisters, closer to her in some ways but often a step removed from the day-to-day grind of treatments, the increasing pain, the decreasing hope, and so on, were resistant to her desire to let go of the effort. Still, Beth has recently made the choice to end treatment, knowing that her death will surely come in a matter of weeks.

A watershed moment between her and one of her sisters came shortly after that decision was made. The sister had taken Beth to a doctor's appointment. The waiting room was the same one she'd sat in when she had gone for her chemotherapy infusions, and as she looked around at the other people who were awaiting their treatments, she turned to her sister and said: "I'm so glad I'm not doing that anymore."

Her sister looked at her in wide-eyed surprise. But from Beth's telling, I think behind those eyes, a light went on.

It was time. It was nearly the end. It was hard. It was okay.

S.

Berlin, Germany (not Berlin, NH ☺)

18 September 2011

Dear Steve,

These topics we're discussing, they're not abstract for me—not that I thought you would take them that way. I'm now writing to you from Berlin where, as I mentioned in my last e-mail, I've come to run a study-abroad program for Dartmouth. Just prior to coming here, my husband and I visited in London with my brother-in-law, Steve; my sister, Maria; and my niece, Francesca (my older niece was already back at university). Steve is mainly incredibly clearheaded and speaks and thinks—and tells good jokes—just like the Steve I've known for decades. The physical reality is that he can barely move about, even with much assistance. My sister tells me that there are now tumors all over his body. He doesn't complain about the injustice of having this rare disease, but his pain is sometimes so bad that it causes him to scream out. I'm still under the shock of hearing those screams and seeing him so reduced. On the one hand, he and my sister are taking important, concrete steps to prepare for the life of the family after he is gone. (While I was there, I had to sign many papers related to guardianship of the child who is still minor, should her mother also pass, and to the family's legal and financial affairs.) On the other, Steve continues to talk about managing to eat more so he can get stronger and walk again, and he refuses to let Maria get a hospital bed for him, which, among other things, would allow for more assistance from the National Health Service. Our departure felt particularly confusing, as Steve didn't seem to want to say good-bye in any way that acknowledged that this could be the last time we see each other, so it certainly didn't seem right that we try to do so.

I have not read the *New Yorker* article you're talking about, and I'll gladly borrow your copy when I'm back in the States. Still, you've recounted it well enough that from your description and from other reading I've done, I believe I understand what alarmed you about the writer's attitude. When you wrote that maybe deaths of children (and death in general) should not be thought of in terms of justice, that maybe asking whether death is fair or unfair is the wrong question, one of my favorite passages from the New Testament on that topic suddenly came into view, a metaphor I'm using on purpose, because the passage concerns the young man blind from birth to whom Jesus gives sight (John 9:1–41). It's one of the longer gospel lessons, and we Orthodox Christians read it the sixth Sunday after Pascha, or Easter, as most other churches refer to it, when we are still very much in the joyous mode of feasting and when the lessons remind us of the life-giving miracles of Jesus.

In passing by a man blind from birth, the apostles are prompted to ask their teacher about the source of his affliction: "Rabbi, who sinned, this man or his parents, that he was born blind?" The teacher answers: "It was not that this man sinned, or his parents, but that the works of God might be made manifest in him." And then the story continues on to relate how Jesus heals him and how surprised everyone is, for "Never since the world began has it been heard that anyone opened the eyes of a man born blind." Asking about the source of the blindness is not the right question, it turns out. Jesus is not interested in assigning blame or determining who is a victim of what. Rather, he wants his disciples to focus on the purpose of this blindness, and that purpose is to create the possibility for something good to happen, something that will reveal the power and love of God. Further references to this healing elsewhere in the New Testament indicate that it did indeed leave quite an impression on those who witnessed it or were told of it. And of course it gives us that beautiful hymn "Amazing Grace": "Was blind, but now I see."

I realize you and I have different relations to Christianity, yet I believe this story, this principle of not searching for blame but rather for the good, elucidates your reaction to the article in the *New Yorker*, to the father's attitude toward his daughter's suffering and death. He couldn't find any purpose whatsoever to her having cancer; what was made manifest in him was anger, pain, and outrage. You have suggested, in contrast, that some things must have happened as result of her illness that are among the most positive experiences of life: making connections to others, feeling empathy, being able to love more deeply. It's hard for me not to wonder if despite his love and intentions, the father's attitude of only seeing the negative in what was happening to his daughter didn't possibly increase her suffering while she was still alive. The death-and-dying pioneer researcher Elisabeth Kübler-Ross, among many others, reports on how difficult it is for children to die peacefully if they are worried about their parents and their parents' ability to go on after the child's death. Kübler-Ross takes this up in a few different books, like *Living with Death and Dying*, and *On Children and Death*.[7] The lesson I'm taking from Kübler-Ross is that if parents are able to find and share with their sick children some positive aspects of all that is going on and can even say—at an appropriate moment and assuming the child is of an appropriate age— that they, the parents and siblings if there are any, will be okay after the child has died, perhaps children with terminal conditions can have their own fears, of whatever origin, alleviated. We can't be sure, of course.

Here's evidence for a "peace dividend" from another source. I have you to thank for pointing me to Stephen Levine and Ondrea Levine's rich book *Who Dies? An Investigation of Conscious Living and Conscious Dying*.[8] I had some trouble with the Buddhist orientation, but at the same time I appreciated the authors' openness to other spiritual traditions. It certainly sounds as though, in their practice with the dying, they meet the individuals in the mind-sets they are in, not where the Levines think they should be. There are so many moments in *Who Dies?* from which I learned deep lessons, and one of them concerns positive life experiences coming out of great suffering. In what I consider the most effective chapter, Stephen Levine reports about his interactions with dying children at Presbyterian Medical Center's Children's Hospital in New York City. My favorite passage concerns a girl just shy of her twelfth birthday who is dying of leukemia. Levine asks her what she thinks is going to happen: "'Well, I guess I'm going to die and go to heaven. And I'm going to be with Jesus.' I asked her, 'What does that mean?' She said, 'Jesus is fair in heaven, but he's not so fair on earth.'"[9] Levine's first reaction to the child's comment is to surmise that it must reflect her parents' attitudes, and his second is that the child herself must be scared about being entrusted to someone who can be so arbitrary. He engages her further by asking gently how Jesus could be fair in one place and not in another. Immediately she answers, "I'm so sick and I haven't done anything wrong. Why should I be sick? Why should I be dying?"[10]

They continue to talk about how it has been for her at school when she is there sometimes and too weak to attend other times. Levine asks about her relationship with the other children and learns that she has made a special friend, a child who has a withered arm and whom the other children mock. He then says to her: "Look how much more compassionate, how much more open, how much more caring you are than your schoolmates. Isn't that all because of your sickness, which you say Jesus gave to you? So this openheartedness, this kindness and love you feel for people that has come out of your illness, is it a tragedy? Or is it somehow, in some remarkable way, a gift of love, a gift of caring that sensitizes you as others seem not to be?"[11] Levine doesn't seem to consider the possibility that this particular child was always sensitive to others. Still, as reported in this book, the child's face lit up upon hearing Levine's analysis, and she responded, "Jesus is fair on earth. Jesus is fair in heaven."[12] Levine concludes this section by reporting that the little girl died peacefully a few weeks later on her birthday. Unfortunately, he doesn't tell us whether the parents, too, were able to undergo a transformation in attitude, to have their worst fears and anger alleviated. Specifically, I wonder if the daughter's peace with her own death helped them accept the loss. Or, I wonder, if the parents had been more at peace, would their attitude have aided the child more or sooner?

Please don't get me wrong. The last thing I would want to do is to criticize the parents of dying children or, for that matter, any person losing a loved one. I have done a lot of grieving in my life, including for the Zantops and for the children I hoped to have and was never able to conceive. As you've seen in our exchanges, I'm anticipating the loss of three major relationships in my life, of my father, my mother-in-law, and my brother-in-law. Mainly, I try to use all that pain to sensitize myself to the suffering of others. So, I don't see my observations as criticism of how others are dealing with their pain and losses, but rather—and following your line of reasoning—I find myself pondering if the fairness issue doesn't lead some of us down the wrong path in thinking about mortality. I don't think Jesus "gave" the cancer to that child, to my brother-in-law, or to anyone else; illness and death were never meant to be in God's divine plan, as far as I understand it. For me the issue is this: once serious illness and mortality are in the picture, what attitude do we hold toward them? What do we do in their presence? To get back to the story of Jesus's gift of sight to the blind man, I wonder if the question we're meant to ask—always and in any situation—is: What is the good that could be happening here and now, and what can my role be in trying to realize that good? What can be made manifest in me or in someone else as a result of this situation? In line with what Levine tells that dying child: Can I think of mortality as a gift?

This brings me to children and adults dying what might indeed be considered unjust deaths, because they are premature deaths due to violence or poverty that were not inevitable. I don't ultimately care about labels. That is, I'm okay with shifting attention from the injustice of it, if, and only if, when we hear or read about such situations, we try to do something to prevent similar deaths from happening again. I can't let myself off the hook. Even if there is nothing I can do for some specific person or persons, I really do need to do something to alleviate hunger or aggression, to promote health and peace, somewhere in the world. As Zulu–South African AIDS activist Xolani Nkosi Johnson told ABC's Jim

Wooten and anyone else he got the chance to speak with before his premature death at age twelve (and weighing just twenty pounds): "Do all you can with what you have in the time you have in the place you are."[13]

To return to your original framework, though, what if our role is to switch the issue from justice to "just death," as in "this is just death"; "this is just the end of a life/my life/your life"? What if instead of asking, *Why should I be dying now?* we asked, *In what fashion am I choosing to die, or to be in the presence of this dying of my loved one?*

It seems to me that when we can truly accept the inevitability of mortality, it is possible to do some very important things. One can speak truth to the situation by saying: I am so sad; I wish this were not happening; I will miss you so much; thank you; I love you; and farewell. If we pretend we ourselves or the loved one near us is not dying, these sentiments are less likely to get expressed out loud to the person or persons who need to hear them. I suspect there are stories in every family, as there are in my own, of someone giving everybody else the command not to tell grandma (grandpa, mom, dad, cousin, uncle, aunt, etc.) she is dying of cancer, because it will scare her. From your work I bet you know a lot about the physical sensations people feel who are close to their deaths. I assume it feels pretty different from health and even from previous stages of their illnesses. For that reason, I can only imagine that when one's most beloved family members and friends deny the imminence of death or act like the problem is something one will lick soon, it can be distressingly confusing to the dying person, like the confusion for the girl dying of leukemia about how Jesus could be fair and unfair at the same time.

Here's another life experience related to what I'm suggesting could be our reaction to dying; it illustrates the point from the other perspective, so to speak. One day, some precious friends of mine from church seemed very sad. When I asked what was wrong, they explained that they had just been told that a close friend of theirs was dead from melanoma. In principle, they could accept that his life was over, but they were devastated because this friend had told no one of his diagnosis and had suffered and died alone. "If only he had shared this news with us," they said to me, "we would so joyfully have taken care of him. He denied himself comfort and us the chance to show him how much we loved him." Who knows what went through that gentleman's head and why he said nothing, but surely from the way my friends experienced it, an opportunity to manifest the human capacity for concern and love had been missed. Even more poignantly, an opportunity for them to say they loved him, and for him to hear it, had been missed. Getting a chance to say good-bye aids the grieving process and certainly at least anecdotally seems to ease the process of dying, too.

You've written several times that Beth has mainly been quite cognizant and accepting of the idea that her life will end soon. Is that allowing her to say her farewells and to accept the farewells of others? At what point do you try to say farewell to your clients?

i.

Cornish, NH
October 8, 2011

Dear Irene,

Beth died a few days ago. I saw her often in her last couple of weeks, including just a day or so before her death. She was increasingly sedated and occasionally delusional during that time, but it was only in the last visit that I wasn't sure she knew who I was. Her husband told me that while her anxiety was sometimes high, she was not in a lot of pain and remained aware of her home and family until close to the end. As late as the second-to-last time I saw her, a few days before she died, she was still smiling and even joking a little.

I never said good-bye to her while she was awake. Each of my last several visits could have been the last, something we both knew and had talked about. I think that that awareness was in her eyes and in mine each time I left. The last visit came after her husband called to tell me that she was getting close. I gave her a gentle massage while stretched out on her bed alongside her. There was no laughing this time. I recall that she smiled a little, but her eyes were not clear and her mind was elsewhere, maybe in transition. When I left, I did what I often do in that situation. I kissed her on the forehead, said "Travel safely," and stepped quietly from the room.

In all the time I knew her, I never heard a single complaint about her bad luck, about the unfairness of someone so full of life getting terminal cancer. That comment of hers I shared with you about being pulled from life came as an answer to a specific question from me when she was at a low point and may have reflected part of the evolution of her thinking. It was not a complaint.

Telling you about Beth reminds me of another client I worked with very closely in the last eight months of her life. Ann was a college fundraiser, in her fifties, who decided late in 2010 to end treatment for her colon cancer because the chemotherapy was having negative side effects and no benefits. Her immediate family was not on board at first, but she had no doubts. She told me often that she believed her body was just a vessel for a life that would carry on in some fashion after that body was gone. Her mother had lectured internationally on the end of life and the afterlife, and had even worked with Kübler-Ross, so Ann was comfortable with contemplating mortality.

Still, her illness was hard despite all she knew and believed. She cried often during our visits as she considered the losses her death would bring: losing her husband, two young-adult kids, other family members, and her large circle of friends. And them losing her. She worried about them. Sometimes, she asked me to tell her how others I had known with her type of cancer fared at the end, to help her visualize what might happen. She provided me many lessons (even helping me figure out how to be a better fundraiser for Hand to Heart), but a particularly important one that I continue to find in my visits with people who are sick or dying is that preparing well and accepting death and mortality, for all their important benefits, won't necessarily make dying easy.

Ann never seemed to consider her cancer or her death a matter of fairness or justice. Whenever death came, she said, she would move on to whatever was next for her. More than most people I have worked with through the massage program, Ann wanted to talk about what was happening and to share her feelings. One of my greatest regrets, in fact, involves that willingness on her part. I visited with her one day when she wasn't feeling up to being on the massage table, so she received the massage while on a bed in a guest room. She was awake, reasonably comfortable, and in good spirits. Our conversation covered a lot of ground, but we both had more to say when the session was over. As I was leaving and making a plan for the next visit, she told me she would look forward to it because she'd been wanting to tell me about her "shifting perception of light." That sounded fascinating to me, and I told her I had some questions for her, so I as well would be eagerly awaiting our next visit.

Alas, when I returned two or three days later, Ann had slipped into a state of mostly sleeping, just awake enough to acknowledge me and smile, but not enough to converse. I remember thinking that that wasn't particularly fair.

Your observation that when people around someone who is dying accept—possibly embrace—what is happening, it might make things easier on the dying person is well supported by studies in the field, I think, and by my own observations of households I visit through Hand to Heart. Many people have confided to me that their anxiety about death is made worse by a husband or wife or mother or father unwilling to even discuss the topic, which might sound familiar to you, given your recent experience with your brother-in-law.

One day, years before I founded The Hand to Heart Project, I ran into a woman I knew only casually, while shopping in a grocery store. She lived in my town and had been in treatment for breast cancer for a few years. This day, she was rail thin, wearing a kerchief, and moving slowly. I expected we would just say hello, exchange pleasantries, and move on. But my "How are you?" brought a long answer that led to a longer conversation, and forty-five minutes passed with us standing in a supermarket aisle, discussing cancer, cancer treatment, insurance, and death. I realized later that she must have been craving such a conversation. I gathered from what she said that she worried about her husband too much to have such talks with him.

Her father was a United Church of Christ minister, and what I learned about him after she had died troubled me. He had come to New Hampshire from Florida for what would turn out to be his last visit with her. It was clear she was dying, but he would say nothing about it. And when he left—surely knowing he wouldn't see her again—he would do no more than give her a smile and a wave, saying something like, "See you soon."

Thank heavens she had several close friends who cared for her with her husband. Still, I can only imagine that her end was more difficult because her father could not accept it. While I won't say that her death at an early age—she was in her forties—was unjust, I could be persuaded to say that that part of it was.

I suspect that the fair/unfair, or just/unjust question is one that has no answer except the one we give it at the time we ask it. Although, as we both have said, there are opportunities for good and for growth to be found even in pain and distress. Still, I wouldn't fault anyone for asking such questions about death. In her book *Being with Dying*, Buddhist priest and teacher Joan Halifax, whose CDs I lent you last winter, relates part of an ancient Hindu story: "Virtuous King Yudhistara (the son of Yama, the Lord of Death) is asked, 'What is the most wondrous thing in the world?' And Yudhistara replies: 'The most wondrous thing in the world is that all around us, people can be dying and we don't believe it can happen to us.'"[14]

Considering that human truth, it shouldn't come as a surprise that so many of us find so little that's fair about our inevitable end.

S.

Berlin
3 November 2011

Dear Steve,

I am deeply sorry for your loss. Please forgive me for not writing sooner. I've just returned from a six-day trip with the students to Dresden and Vienna, and it involves quite a bit of planning and executing on my end. No time for many of my own thoughts.

I've been thinking about Beth and, based on what you'd already written me, I had to assume that she might die soon. I realize that to effectively do the work you do with the dying, you must have learned to function without your emotions overwhelming you. Yet by the same token, to be there as a human presence for individuals in pain, for individuals who are facing the greatest mystery of life, you must also have cultivated an ability to be emotionally available to them. So, as much as the words of your last letter sound calm and measured, I read behind them a sense of loss. I hope it comforts you to recall what concrete help you offered Beth and Ann and all the others. I refer to your talent with touch, of course, but also to your open ears, and mind, and heart.

You've amassed lots of proof that I'm loquacious. Yet I will be the first to admit that in trying to respond to someone who has just experienced the death of a loved one, I am typically tongue-tied or lame in the fingers that usually type and write so quickly. Ever since losing Susanne and Half Zantop, however, I always try to say or write something to the bereaved. You see, the silence of those friends and acquaintances who said absolutely nothing to me in the wake of the Zantops' murders was excruciatingly painful. Sometimes it actually felt like their silence was physically hurting me. I quickly realized that it was much more reassuring when individuals said something—no matter how awkward—than when they acted like nothing had happened. So, when I hear that someone has died, I push myself to write to those suffering the loss. Even if I rarely have the sense that the content is "right," I hope the gesture might be.

In my church community, we keep lists of names of individuals for whom we and in turn the priest and the community pray. One list concerns those for whom we pray for healing and comfort and the other for those who have fallen asleep, as dying is often referred to in our faith, since we believe they will awake at the Second Coming. I'll add you to the first and Beth to the second.

Be well, dear friend. I hope to write to you again before too long.

Irene

CHAPTER 3

HOW DO I HANDLE PAIN AT END OF LIFE?

Berlin

5 December 2011

Dear Steve,

The last weeks of the program I lead in Berlin are always filled with even more activities than usual, as there are the proverbial end-of-the semester assignments, projects, and tests to explain and correct. And in the midst of all that, there's Thanksgiving and our local tradition of celebrating it with the host families and the students. I typically do the coordinating and a fair amount of the cooking for the fifty-plus people. This year, because of the scheduling, we also had events related to Advent, a particularly cherished season for most Germans, with outdoor markets, special food and drink, and lots of visits with family and friends. Well, at 9 a.m. today, the program was officially over. As much as I enjoy the teaching and my students—and the young people in the group this year were particularly pleasant and cooperative—I found myself staring at the clock, waiting for 9 a.m. to arrive. When it did, I gave thanks that we all made it through healthy, and then, breathing a deep sigh of relief, let it sink in that I am no longer responsible for their welfare.

I believe that this year, that morning breath was even deeper than usual since I have a lot to process emotionally. Last week, on top of all the expected foreign-study program events, my sister Maria asked me to come to London so that we could go to the premier of *Hugo*, a movie our sister Georgia had produced. Given the strain Maria and the girls have been under this year with her husband's almost total dependence, and with being told by his doctors several different times that he's about to die, I immediately agreed to come. Without much trouble, I was able to reschedule a class and book a flight from Berlin to London to be with them for two days. (Places seem so much closer in Europe!) We got very dressed up and had a lot of fun, among other things finding ourselves seated very close to Prince Charles and Camilla; the movie's director, Martin Scorsese; and dozens of other celebrities, including one I actually recognized, Rod Stewart. I'm not much of a celebrity stalker actually, but it made me so happy to know that Maria and my younger niece—the older one was back at university—were out of the house and engrossed in that festive atmosphere, even if for only a few hours. The movie itself transported me. While it's always a thrill to see our sister's name on the big screen, in such company it was especially fun.

What a contrast that glamour and the fantasy of the movie itself provided to what is going on in their home. Maria had arranged for Steve's favorite nurse to spend the evening with him, and fortunately no crises arose while we were gone—none like the night before, when Steve experienced excruciating pain and began screaming. The screaming had continued through most of the night, at least to the point when I finally managed to fall asleep. I suppose you've been in such situations. I knew screaming, or something akin to it, from my Dad, also a man with a big voice, from the transfers during his rehab stay. I already knew what my brother-in-law's shouting sounded like from that previous visit at the end of the summer I told you about. But never had I heard a sound like this. We say metaphorically all the time: "it sounded like he was being tortured," but that doesn't strike me as an adequate description for what I was hearing. The poor guy; I can only assume it was more pain than he'd ever felt before, the way he was vocalizing it. Now a lay person like me would assume that someone whose body is filled with tumors would be receiving adequate pain medication. And it turns out, my brother-in-law could have it anytime he wants. Their house is filled with meds. "Wanting to," though; that's precisely the glitch in this situation.

We never know what's truly going on inside of another human being, but as far as I can tell from what he says out loud, there's a part of Steve that still hangs on to the idea of healing, of beating this disease. The afternoon I arrived, he and I were conversing in the couple's bedroom—transformed since my last visit at the end of the summer into a sickroom with a proper hospital bed and accoutrements—and Steve told me he needed to eat more so that he could regain his strength and get out of bed. On some level, I suppose most of us would automatically salute this attitude as life-affirming and positive. I have trouble doing so because he connects resuming a normal life with refusing adequate pain medication. The current physical reality, I've been told, is that there are so many tumors in his body, and they are impinging on so many of his vital systems, that not only will he not walk again, his death is also very near. You will know better than I what kind of pain tumors can cause. When my brother-in-law's pain hits a certain level, he starts screaming, and then it usually takes until the arrival of a qualified member of the National Health Service to give him a shot of morphine before he can calm down and be more comfortable. As attentive as the NHS has been to him, that can still mean a few hours of excruciating pain for him and the sound of his screaming for everyone within earshot. (The situation brought to mind the dying of Malte Laurids Brigge's grandfather in Rilke's novel we shared thoughts about a few months ago: everyone in the vicinity was subject to it.)

That's the scenario that unfolded during my visit with my London family last week, before we went to the premiere. I'm not sure how Steve and Maria made the decision, but at some point during that night of pain and screaming, Steve had finally agreed to let Maria place a call to the NHS and she did so. The team arrived in the morning. While I was making myself a cup of tea in the kitchen to try to stay out of their way, four women caretakers—National Health Service nurses and aides—

plus my sister Maria attended to Steve. He's a tall man. Come to think of it, you two share not only a first name but also a height category. So even though my brother-in-law has lost a lot of weight, it is difficult to lift and turn him, especially now that he can't assist. They bathed him, changed his pajamas and robe, and one of them gave him morphine. Over the course of the next several hours, calm returned to their home. And we eventually went out and had that fun evening I described. Only, the echoes of Steve's pain were very much with me in the movie theater, and I assume with Maria and my niece, too.

I believe it would be upsetting to just about anyone to hear the sound of someone in so much pain. I was and still am feeling a lot of sadness. And plenty of confusion. It is hard for me not to wonder about Steve's refusal of pain medication until the level of pain gets so bad that it causes that kind of screaming. Pondering justice, as you and I have, I also find myself wondering about Steve's right to do what he thinks he needs to do to stay alive, to keep himself motivated to stay alive, and about the cost that others, particularly my sister and my teenage niece still living at home—and for that matter, my older niece, who's interrupted her studies to return home several times when the doctors thought her father's death was imminent—might be paying as a consequence of the choices he is claiming for himself. I feel like I must be an awful human being to write such a thought, even as I know I am being honest.

It won't surprise you that I find myself ruminating about life with death, about what difference it might make to this situation if Steve were able to accept the fact of his own mortality. My sister has been urging her husband to write letters to their two daughters, letters that they might perhaps read when they graduate from university, marry, or experience some other occasion in the future when he won't be around, and they will surely be thinking about him and what it would be like for them if he were there. According to what my sister reports, Steve refuses to try to compose such messages, because that would indicate that he'd given up. It seems to me that there's a key to a larger issue for all of us in

Steve's behavior: what would it take for an individual or a whole culture to *not equate* the reality of mortality with defeat, with giving up on life? What articulation is needed to think of acknowledging that we die *as an embrace of life itself*? Accepting one's impending death could free one to do some things that couldn't be more life-affirming, for instance, to demonstrate one's love for one's spouse and kids. In the case of my family, that might mean consciously choosing to act out of love for others by taking more medication or writing letters. I feel a real urgency to try to express this coherently. Does my logic make sense here? Can you see conscious acknowledgment of our mortality as leading to an embrace of life itself?

Irene

Cornish, NH
December 12, 2011

Dear Irene,

Sure it does. A lot about the story you told in that letter is familiar, and much of it makes sense—including your brother-in-law's decisions, even if I would wish them to be different. Wish as I will, though, I can't truly fathom what's going on for him. As you wrote, we can never know what exactly is going on inside another person, which brings to my mind something that John O'Donohue wrote in his book *Anam Cara*: "There is the solitude of suffering, when you go through darkness that is lonely, intense, and terrible. Words become powerless to express your pain; what others hear from your words is so distant and different from what you are actually suffering."[1]

These are interesting trains of thought to be traveling in the Christmas season, aren't they? I haven't been an enthusiastic celebrator of Christmas for quite a few years, but with two young granddaughters now, it feels a little more special, and a little more joyful. Having Molly and Sawyer to think about also seems to lighten the heavier, sometimes-challenging mix of thoughts that come with our contemplations about death and dying.

A lot of progress has been made in the treatment of pain in the last decade or two. It wasn't all that long ago that medical schools didn't include much training in pain management. Many physicians apparently considered pain, even extreme pain, a natural consequence of disease that patients simply had to endure. Pain drugs are more sophisticated now, and medical practitioners are more likely to see pain as something that needs to be treated. Here is one fact about pain that Steve might be missing when he makes the decision to opt out of strong medications: It is a lot easier to prevent pain from happening than it is to knock it down once it has flared.

And yet, extraordinary pain—"breakthrough" pain, as it is sometimes called in chronic-pain sufferers—does sometimes require drugs that leave one feeling muddled or sleepy or out of it. That is not true as often as it used to be; many people's end-of-life pain can be managed these days without sedating them into semi or complete unconsciousness. But that's not the case for everyone. In more than a few situations, modern pain management isn't able to help without resorting to heavy sedation, and deciding to accept that will be seen by some people as giving up. I can see why. People with life-threatening or life-ending disease have to make a lot of transitions they'd rather not make. Giving up a job. Giving up driving. Adjusting to a new body image. Giving up the various roles one has in various relationships. One of the biggest transitions must be letting oneself be medicated into less awareness. It's not like going under anesthesia for surgery, with the expectation that you'll be awake again soon. It must feel like nothing less than releasing one's hold on life and personal identity.

As much as I can sympathize with the dying person in pain, though, I also understand what you are saying about the impact such suffering can have on the people nearby, especially family. How hard must it be to hear your husband or father bellowing in pain? How seemingly simple a thing for the sufferer to accept medication that would spare his loved ones that experience? The "death with dignity" or "right to die" movement includes many people who want the right to choose their time of death if they have an incurable illness not just so that they can avoid the experience of severe end-of-life pain themselves, but also to spare loved ones from watching what Steve's family is watching.

I remember talking years ago with Ira Byock, palliative-care physician and author, about this topic.[2] It was back in my newspaper days, and I was interviewing him for an article about Vermont's "death with dignity" movement. He was not a fan of pending right-to-die legislation, not because he thought people should be left to suffer in their final days, but because—and I'm paraphrasing here, of course—he saw that legislation as an easy way out. End-of-life care needed vast improvement, he told me, and focusing on allowing people to end their lives with medical help takes the focus away from the need to properly staff nursing homes so that residents are not left unfed, uncleaned, and unmedicated; to better support families who are caring for dying loved ones; and to better train doctors on how to understand and treat pain. I don't imagine that anything leads dying people to want to end life "early" more than does terrible pain. Do better with that, and the end of life will surely be transformed for many people.

I have a massage-therapy client who has thought a lot about that very point since she is dealing with a cancer that she knows will end her life, possibly soon. She has adult children who—she wouldn't say this, but I've picked it up from some of her stories—are not entirely in tune with what is happening to her. As a result, they haven't been a lot of help in her effort to plan for how she will die, and she worries that her approach to death will be very difficult for them. She does not want to be in a lot of pain, and she does not want her family to see her in a lot of pain. Pain seems to be what she fears most about dying—more than the dying itself.

This is all background for the story she told me one day more than a year ago when she arrived for an appointment. "I've finally figured out a way to kill myself without leaving a big mess for everyone to deal with," she said.

"You have?" I asked.

Here is what she told me: She lives near a large wooded area where she often walks with her dog. She said that when the time came (meaning when she thought it time to end her life on her own terms), she planned to go off the path a bit and dig a big hole. She would suspend ropes and pulleys from a tree overhanging the hole, tying large bags of dirt to the ends of the ropes at one side, and larger, heavier blocks of ice to the other ends. Then she'd get in the hole—maybe into a plastic bag to make things even neater—and take whatever she would take to end her life. Slowly, the ice would melt, allowing the bags to tip up and dump the dirt on top of her. Death and burial, both taken care of in one step. It was a plan worthy of Rube Goldberg.

Of course, I thought I had her because I could spot a few problems with her plan. I almost pointed out that if it was winter, the ice might not melt. And how would she get those big bags of dirt, enough to fill that big hole, into the air in just the right spot? Instead, I noted only that when the time came for her to take a big step like that, she probably wouldn't be in any condition to dig a hole in the woods.

"You're right," she said thoughtfully. "I'd better start now."

The fantastical nature of the plan notwithstanding, she obviously had been trying to picture how she would die, and what effect that process would have on her and her family. Avoiding pain was a big part of the picture for her. She wanted to avoid it for herself, and for the people who would see her experiencing it. Months later, in a less fanciful moment, she told me after a massage appointment that she was headed off to have an MRI to see if the cancer had spread to her brain. I asked her to let me know the results, and she replied that if I didn't hear anything, the results probably were good. If they were bad, she'd be back soon to say good-bye.

"Well, geez," I said. "It probably won't happen all that fast."

She responded that if they told her she needed more radiation or chemotherapy to slow a brain metastasis, she would say her good-byes and take pills she had stashed away for just that purpose, probably in the presence of some close friends she knew would care for her. There was a problem with this plan, too, however. She had recently moved from one condo to another, smaller one, and everything was still packed in boxes. She couldn't remember where her stash was.

I don't mean to make light of pain, especially intense pain at the end of life. Losing life is probably the biggest transition we'll make, even if we don't know what the other side of the transition is. Most of us will find it intimidating, and a little or a lot frightening. In the midst of that turmoil, add tremendous pain. Is it possible that the two together are worse because they *are* together, that the whole is more than the sum of the parts? Would the same amount of pain in a non-life-threatening condition—maybe shingles, or a bad fracture—be easier to cope with because recovery is assumed?

If so, that would bring us back to the potential benefit of shifting our relationship to mortality. If pain is worse when it is part of an anxious and difficult approach to death, would it be more tolerable if that approach were not so anxious and difficult? If we accept death more easily and gracefully, would we perhaps feel less pain?

Steve

P.S. I have a book called *Handbook for Mortals* written by two doctors; it's very helpful on this subject of pain, as on many others.[3] It's actually written as a sort of workbook, with a lot of information and suggestions that might demystify death and dying for readers, and it offers many practical tips on how to manage your own approaching death, or that of someone close to you. I can lend it to you if you'd like.

Lebanon, NH
Saturday, 17 December 2011

Dear Steve,

Well, we are now once again only about twenty miles apart. I hope that means we'll talk face-to-face soon. However, with me still trying to unpack my bags—just got back to the USA Thursday night—and the holidays upon us, I assume that won't be right away. I hope you'll let me continue the conversation by e-mail. Plus, this feels rather familiar by now. For you, too?

I want to thank you from the bottom of my heart for your thoughts of 12 December. They were profoundly helpful to me, especially the ones about what decisions to take pain medications might feel like to the sufferers. I now see more clearly what you're saying about all the major transitions people with debilitating or terminal illness face and how each of those transitions can feel like a major loss. With our three family invalids (and alas, several friends, too) experiencing major pain and probably soon their mortal ends, I think it will be important for me to develop deeper knowledge and sympathy about what life feels like for them now. I should be asking myself more frequently what might be the causes for behaviors they are displaying, decisions they are making, or things they are saying. And thanks for the offer of loaning me that book. What a great title: *Handbook for Mortals*! I'll try to remind you to bring it along when we finally figure out a time to visit in person.

I just found out that my brother-in-law has had a port inserted into his body. Again, I suspect you understand a lot more about this than I do. What I got from my sister is that a device was implanted that allows pain medication to be delivered more directly and therefore more effectively and faster. I gather, too, that my sister can administer doses of strong painkillers without having to wait for medical personnel to arrive. A lot of that sounds like progress to me, especially based on what you said about the importance of preventing pain from getting out of control in the first place. Yet, if Steve agreed to the port, this must also mean that he had reached the point where he was in even more pain. And of course this makes me very sad indeed. Does it also mean that he has accepted the idea that he is dying? I don't know.

The story about your client and her plan to "self-bury" made me laugh, for which I am grateful. We've done precious little laughing in the family lately. She sure is likely to have trouble digging a hole and having ice melt around here in New England at least six months of the year. No matter how impractical the solution and how regrettable I find suicide, I admire her desire to think through her own death in advance in a way that includes its consequences for those she loves.

I also appreciate your query about whether acceptance of the general idea of death or the specific imminence of one's own death might affect how pain is experienced. Your train of thought led me to remember other New Englanders who have given me ideas about what I might choose for myself if I learn that my death is likely near. Interestingly, like your client, they are strangers to me, and yet I feel they've modeled ends I will try to emulate if the circumstances allow. The first was "Mike," the elderly husband of an administrator at Dartmouth. I couldn't tell you the exact year he died, but it must have been more than ten years ago, because Susanne Zantop was still alive. I learned from her about the decision Mike had made to discontinue any treatments, stay at home, and stop eating. As I understood it, he said his good-byes to his children and friends, and with his wife moistening his lips or giving liquids as he desired, he simply got weaker and weaker until he passed away.

I learned the story of the other individual from our local public-radio station. A daughter recounted her mother's end-of-life sequence. The mother had had a stroke, been transported to the hospital, and received treatment there, which she experienced as painful and unnecessary. I don't remember any of the actual details that might explain why she felt that way about her treatment. What I do remember clearly is that when she returned to her own home, she talked it over with all members of her family and had them post signs around the house, including near the telephones, that stated that if she had another stroke or other major physical breakdown, she was not to be resuscitated nor taken to the hospital. I don't remember if they used some standard "Do Not Resuscitate" language or if they made up their own. But the signs made clear that she did not want to enter the medical environment again; she wanted to die at home. Here's what happened. She had a few relatively pain-free, comfortable weeks in which she said her good-byes, and then another stroke occurred. She was conscious but couldn't speak. She looked into her daughter's eyes to make sure the daughter knew she was still determined to stay put and let the stroke take its course. She died right there at home, as she wished.

I'm sure that you and many others, including doctors, could report on the unpredictability of any individual's end. Still, the kernel I'm seeing in your anecdote and my two is that the three individuals involved had truly wrapped their minds around the idea of their mortal lives ending, including how their condition while dying might affect their loved ones. In each case, that thought permitted courses of action to be contemplated, the mere contemplation of which seems to have engendered peaceful feelings. At least that's how Mike's and the anonymous woman's deaths were reported. It seems to me that if your client can be so lighthearted, concretely thinking through her own death must have had a calming effect on her, too. Whether that peace translated into less physical pain for those individuals, or is doing so for your client, I do not know. However, in neither of the two stories I heard did the survivors speak about the dying person being in excruciating pain. Come to think of it, they didn't mention pain in the last phase at all, whereas they did emphasize peace.

I guess I'll be hearing from Maria about whether the port—or a concomitant acceptance of his impending death?—is helping Steve in the peace department. I sure hope so. For his sake. And for his family's.

Yours,
Irene

Cornish, NH
December 22, 2011

Dear Irene,

I have such a hard time imagining what it must be like to be in really serious pain. I have cracked and separated a shoulder in a motorcycle accident; later had surgery to remove part of my collar bone; sprained each ankle more than a dozen times, sometimes very badly; ruptured the patella tendon below my left knee so that my kneecap ended up halfway up my thigh; broken a wrist; had several other minor to moderate surgeries; and I was knocked around by my older brother many times as a kid (a birth-order requirement, I believe). Still, I don't think I have a clue what it is like to have intense pain that lasts and lasts and lasts.

I once had a massage-therapy client who has multiple sclerosis; lupus, which can cause significant muscle and joint pain; and fibromyalgia, a not-well-understood condition that also comes with severe pain. She usually rated her daily pain level at a six or seven on a zero-to-ten scale, with spikes to the top of the scale. Six or seven is considered very high. No one who doesn't have that routine experience of pain can imagine what it is like, I'm sure. How can it be possible to move through one's day with such pain and accomplish anything, never mind with a good nature or a smile?

It's a rhetorical question, because I know that it can be done. This particular client, in fact, did it all the time. She'd had surgeries, falls, and other incidents to add to her chronic conditions, and yet when she was on my massage table, she was likely to be telling stories about her son, her parents, and her nieces and nephews. Usually positive, upbeat stories.

I'm also thinking right now of two clients I've been seeing through Hand to Heart, both of whom have been dealing with severe pain. One is a woman in her late thirties who has a rare genetic disorder that predisposes her to tumors, some cancerous, and specifically to breast cancer, which she has had. She lives with her young daughter and has the most positive attitude you can imagine, despite the fact that she experiences major headaches all the time. Every time I call to see about scheduling a massage visit, she sounds happy. It's only when I quiz her a little about how she's doing that I get details revealing how much pain she is in. She'll tell me about it, and then she'll put it aside, saying it's manageable, and that she's focusing on raising her daughter, not thinking about how she feels. That outward focus—wanting or needing to care for someone else—must be part of how she copes. She obviously doesn't want her pain to affect her daughter's life any more than is necessary.

The other person is a woman in her sixties who cannot catch a break from her ovarian cancer. Whenever she thinks it's faded to the background, it surges forward again, causing intense pain in her abdomen, frequently requiring hospitalization to bring it under control. Yet she gives a wonderful spin on the idea of having something to live for. In her case, it's not about something to live for indefinitely, as I suspect she knows that her time is fairly short. It's about something to live for right now. She treasures her life with her husband and kids, and her first grandchild is on the way. I can almost hear her asking: What is pain next to those things?

One answer to that question—to change the direction of this train of thought—is that pain is a form of suffering, and suffering is something we each share with all other beings. It connects us to each other as much as Earth's air and water do. We yearn for happiness, and sometimes we get it. But it's always fleeting, and that is often the basis for our suffering. What do we do with that?

I've found one answer in the notion of connecting my own difficulties, my suffering and pain, to the wide universe of suffering and pain. They are part of my life, and they are part of all life. I'm not alone when I blow out my knee and have intense pain; I share that experience with everyone else. I won't be alone when I'm dying and in pain, either. Perhaps I can even think of my suffering as possibly easing the suffering of someone else; my intention and compassion could be like a prayer for whoever needs it.

Perhaps. This is a quite-selfless way to approach pain, and especially death, and I have no idea if I'll be up to such selflessness when my time comes. But we don't need to wonder what effect it *could* have, do we? We can look at my clients and see that a young girl is growing up with a mother who won't let pain keep her from being a mother. And that a pregnant young woman and her husband have a bright and positive force in their lives, the grandmother-to-be, even in the face of her great pain and approaching end of life. We also can guess that your sister and her daughters would be suffering your brother-in-law's last days or weeks less intensely if he could see his life, his death, and his pain in this way. It's not a criticism of how he is approaching his end. But maybe it's an opportunity for those around him and those of us who hear his story to think about how they might learn from his experience and shift their own thinking.

Anyway, welcome back to New Hampshire. You haven't missed much of a winter so far. I'm sure we'll plan to meet in person again soon, but with the holidays and our busy schedules, I agree that that can wait a bit. Until then, these e-mail exchanges are proving to be helpful ways for me to develop my thoughts about life, death, and life with death. So by all means, let's keep them going.

Steve

White Plains, NY
27 December 2011

Dear Steve,

I am hoping more than ever to visit with you again soon in person, but I thought you would want to know right away that my brother-in-law in London passed away on Christmas Day. He had a long, long journey with his disease. Maria and both their daughters were with him when he passed, and Maria said he looked at peace.

It could seem a rather-awful legacy to die on Christmas, but the way I see it, Steve was trying to give his family the only gift he had left to bestow, which was not to die on December 24, his younger daughter's birthday. I like the thought of him consciously bestowing a final gift. That's like him. For all I wrote about how he was handling his medication, my brother-in-law was an exceedingly generous person.

Before we learned all this, I had planned to write you that Maria had let me know that while Steve was becoming more and more incoherent, he no longer seemed to be in pain. I am so grateful for his sake and also because his family got to experience him in a "pain-free" state before they lost him. It's an odd coincidence that just before I left Berlin, I saw a film titled *Halt auf freier Strecke* (Stopped on Track) that had many similarities to what went on for my London family, only the man in the film is younger and suffers terminal brain cancer.[4] At one point, the wife-mother thinks she just can't handle the burden of his care at home anymore, and the social worker advises that it would be a shame for the children not to experience him in the next phase, which she promises will be more pain-free, and indeed it is. He dies at home, and his wife and kids calmly say their good-byes and get on with their lives.

Personal experience . . . hmmmm . . . sometimes we'd rather not have it . . .

And yet, what you shared about the attitudes of the young mother and the grandmother-to-be made me very happy and give me hope, actually. Maybe it's not pie-in-the-sky to imagine a peaceful end. Your account of your clients made me remember my precious friend Judy, who had multiple sclerosis and was a quadriplegic in the entire period I knew her. She, too, was cheerful almost all the time. I promise to tell you more about her on another occasion.

As for offering one's pain and suffering to the universe, I saw a moving opera by the French composer Francis Poulenc about nuns killed in the French Revolution, *Dialogues des Carmélites* (Dialogue of the Carmelites).[5] There's a fascinating sequence where the mother prioress is lying on her deathbed in terrible fear and pain, and another nun interprets what's going on as the prioress dying the awful death meant for someone else, so that that other person can die her peaceful death. A fascinating idea, but not self-evident. Maybe we'll need to take that up again sometime, too.

I hope you and Nora are well and had a meaningful Christmas celebration with your granddaughters.

Soon,

Irene

Cornish, NH
December 28, 2011

Irene,

Thank you for letting me know. I'm sorry to hear that your brother-in-law has died. I'm glad to know that his family was with him and that he seemed comfortable. I'm also glad you got to be there at least a couple times in recent months. And you're right about personal experience. Sometimes, it's a little too personal.

My wife's mother was one of the most lively, creative, life-embracing people I've ever known, an accomplished batik artist, and possibly the best grandmother ever. But she outlived her husband by quite a few years and wasn't happy about that. As her health failed, she became almost curmudgeonly at times—highly unlike her, to my prior experience. She even seemed to want to find a way out of her life on occasion. Friends found her on the floor of her home more than once, after she had taken a few too many pills with not enough to eat. I was never sure if she was actually trying to end her life, but I remember telling her once that when she really was facing her certain and imminent death, I would support her if she chose to end it on her own terms. I just didn't think she was at that point yet.

I mention this only because of a conversation her decline sparked with some friends one evening. My wife and I were having dinner with the children's book artist Trina Schart Hyman and her partner, Jean Aull, on a cold winter night at their home. We got to talking about Nora's mother, and the one thing I remember about that conversation is that Trina told Nora, who was having a hard time with her mother's situation, that we always look to our elders to show us how to die. She continued, Nora's mother was not doing it well. That made it hard to watch (it got much harder before she did die), but it was no less a lesson for how Nora, her sisters, and others of us paying close attention, might want to think about our own ends.

Thinking about our deaths. Taking away, if not the mystery, maybe some of the fear, and thereby some of the struggle. In one of his often-quoted essays, sixteenth-century philosopher Michel de Montaigne proposed stealing death's power.

> To begin depriving death of its greatest advantage over us, let us adopt a way clean contrary to that common one; let us deprive death of its strangeness; let us frequent it, let us get used to it. . . . Let us never be carried away by pleasure so strongly that we fail to recall occasionally how many are the ways in which that joy of ours is subject to death or how many are the fashions in which death threatens to snatch it away. . . . We do not know where death awaits us: so let us wait for it everywhere. To practise death is to practise freedom.[6]

A bit florid, perhaps, but chalk it up to the excitability of sixteenth-century essayists. Anyway, best wishes for a fruitful and happy new year, for you and for us.

Steve

Chapter 4

WHAT ABOUT CAREGIVING?

Cornish, NH
Jan. 12, 2012

Dear Irene,

The story of your brother-in-law Steve's last months and his death bring to mind another facet of the end of life: caregiving. Caregivers face so many challenges that they never expected to face. Young couples marrying do not—"till death do us part" notwithstanding—envision that one of them might be feeding, cleaning, medicating, and making decisions for the other at some point. We are not brought up with the understanding that we might do those things for one or both of our parents—not in our culture, at least.

And yet, there we often are, turning our lives upside down to meet the needs of someone whose needs are many, and whose time might be short. I was visiting an elderly fellow last week who has end-stage cancer. His wife, a retired nurse, is caring for him with the help of their children. During my visit he told me that his mother and his wife's mother had both lived with them for extended periods before they died. That might have been typical when that couple was first married decades ago, but it's an uncommon commitment to caring for family these days, wouldn't you say?

It's no wonder that so many people say they don't want to become a burden on those they love. Who would want that? Who would ask someone to give up so much in time, energy, and even money to care for them during what can seem, in advance, an almost-unbearable process?

And who, given a choice, would make the decision to become a caregiver, no matter how much they might want to? I think what's important is that the questions are asked, even if only implicitly. We scatter so far from our early homes and our families of origin that caring for a dying loved one means answering a tough question: Can I do it? It means making difficult choices and sacrifices related to one's career, one's finances, and perhaps to one's own young family.

And so, many people getting close to the end of life will make their own choices that avoid the need for their loved ones to take care of them. They move to facilities that will care for them until they die, or they opt to die in a hospital. If it all works out, no one they know will have to take them in, move in with them, or leave a job or family to be the caregiver.

This reminds me of that friend of mine whom I wrote about earlier—the one who came up with the convoluted plan to, at just the right time, end her life and provide her own burial. No loose ends. That facetious plan was, in part, her way of trying to avoid being a burden on her sons, because she knew that if her dying was protracted and difficult, they would have a hard time managing it. At the same time, she wasn't looking to die alone or in a sterile medical environment. Her ideal was to choose her time, take some pills, and die in the care of several friends she felt would be up to the experience.

I would say she's on the right track, but I still wonder. Here's another possible ideal. Years ago, one of the very first people I worked with through Hand to Heart was a middle-aged woman who lived in an off-the-grid cabin in the hills of Vermont. She lived alone but had a large group of friends who came together to care for her during the last months before she died of cancer. One close friend, who was between jobs, moved in with her and became the primary caregiver, and many others were at the house every day, doing chores, making or bringing food, caring for their dying friend in ways large and small, intimate and mundane. And to hear them talk, at least the few I saw in my visits, it was an honor they would not have passed up for anything.

In his first book, *Dying Well*, Ira Byock, MD, whom I've mentioned before as one of the leading voices in the movement to transform the end-of-life experience, offered many examples of friends and families coming together to help in the last period of a loved one's life. Byock made a strong case for why we should perhaps be willing to allow people to care for us at the end: It is a gift to care for someone you love; it is an honor.[1]

In 2005, I spent some time visiting with and interviewing a woman in her nineties who was nearing her death and wanted to talk about it. We agreed that I'd interview her several times over her last months, and then after she died, I'd produce an article for the local newspaper. Ann Ogden—a different Ann from the one I told you about a few e-mails back—was spirited and had lived much of her life alone, but she had countless friends in many circles. There was the circle of people active in the "death with dignity" movement in Vermont, in which she was prominent. There was her French-speaking social group. She was an artist with a circle of diversely creative friends. She was the kind of person who I'm sure had many friends who didn't know each other because they knew her in just one part of her life. She had little family, and none in the area, but she would not have lacked for people to take care of her as her congestive heart failure took her strength away over several months.

She would have none of it, though. No one would lift her onto or off a toilet. No one would be dressing or feeding her. When she could no longer toddle into the kitchen in the morning to make her poached egg, trailing yards and yards of plastic tube providing oxygen, she would know the time had come. She would make that call herself, and she planned to be alone when she died.

I knew that Ann knew Ira Byock; they had an amiable disagreement over right-to-die legislation being proposed in Vermont.[2] I knew she liked him. I reminded her once of Ira's point that allowing people close to her to care for her at the end might be conferring a great honor on them. She fixed me with a steely look and said, "Well, they're going to have to find somebody else."

In Ann's case, no one asked or got to answer the question. I really liked Ann, and I respected the choices she made. But at the same time, I hope I see it differently when my time comes. I don't expect to have a train of people in and out of my house, singing and doing chores, and keeping me amused and distracted from my discomforts and agitations. Those things, in fact, probably would become my discomforts and agitations. But a few people caring for me when I no longer can seems like a good way to live at the end. And a good way to die.

How's that for a "Happy New Year"?

Steve

Lebanon, NH

Monday, 16 January 2012

Dear Steve,

Well, I'm not so sure about the "Happy New Year" part. To be sure, I'm feeling under the somber shadow of my brother-in-law's death. With all the running around I have to do for my profession at this time of year—going to our biggest and most important conference and starting the new academic term—I can tell I'm not having the quiet moments I need to grieve. I had wanted to fly to London to be with Maria and my nieces, but Maria felt pretty sure she was okay handling this on her own, and we're fortunate that our sister Georgia had already planned a trip over for later this month. Maria's probably as fine as can be expected; I'm beginning to wonder if it isn't I who need to be near her to accomplish my own grieving.

How's this instead of "Happy New Year"? "Here's to a meaningful Martin Luther King, Jr. Day." I bet some of his family wish they'd had a chance to care for him in his old age. He was born the same year as my father and would have turned eighty-three yesterday. Why, he might not even have needed caregivers yet! I don't mean to sound facetious, especially not about one of my true heroes. But by bringing up caretaking, you've brought up a subject that has weighed on me almost constantly—and for years now. You know about my sister and her girls taking care of their Steve for so long. From his diagnosis to his death, it was twelve years. In that time he underwent seven major operations, several minor procedures, and almost countless treatments—standard and experimental, received in three different countries on two different continents. All that plus convalescing each time required a lot of management and caretaking. And he got them. The result was that Steve was able to make rapid recoveries in the first years and retained many physical abilities, including walking. Alas, there was then a cruel, fairly steady decline, and he was pretty much bedridden the last four months of his life. Steve's situation dominated several families' lives, those of his nuclear family, his family of origin, and my family, the family he married into. Why was that? I ask myself. I guess the answer is in part because he was young, in part because the disease and its course are so unfamiliar, and in part because worrying about others is a strong characteristic of our families.

But Steve's illness hasn't been the only thing going on for us. You might remember that my mother-in-law had a stroke in 2004, after which she was never strong enough to live as independently as she had prior to the stroke; and my mom and dad were in a car crash a few months later in January 2005, in the wake of which Dad started at first a slow and then a much more rapid decline. So, members of every part of my family have been caring for other members of my family for years now. Some of us are primary caregivers, like my sister and my mother to their husbands and one of my sisters-in-law to her mother. And many of us are secondary caregivers, taking over for a few hours, days, or weeks when we can, doing supportive work like laundry, cleaning, or cooking when we're around, and—not to be overlooked—providing to our family on the front line a sympathetic ear by phone, by e-mail, or in person, plus distractions or entertainment from a distance or while we're doing substitute caretaking.

Of course my family is not exceptional for being in this situation.

Even with the cultural differences you mention, due to the aging popula-
tion in general and certainly among my friends, more and more people
must figure out how to get the care they need, or how to get it for or give
it to someone they know.

I haven't read the book by Ira Byock that you mention, but I can still
appreciate your and his point about the honor of giving care to someone.
I suppose we're lucky for that sensibility, since otherwise I'm not sure
who would be staffing the hospitals and nursing homes, not to mention
the invisible masses taking care of loved ones in their homes. From my
perspective as a secondary caregiver watching primary caregivers, the
trickiest part for primary caregivers can be renewing one's energy and
commitment, especially when a situation one assumes might last a few
months turns into one that lasts numerous years. I suppose that as a
Greek woman raised in a traditional way, my mother always knew that she
might end up caring for her husband. Still, I remember that as my father
became more demented and especially when he became incontinent, it
was a hard, if not bitter, transition for my mother to realize that her relationship to her competent, hardworking, fun-loving, joke-telling husband
resembled more closely her relationship to her children as very young
infants—except that infants are small, are easy to pick up, and daily gain
skills that will make them independent.

With the elderly and terminally ill, dependence likely just keeps
growing. I know that in my mother-in-law's case, there's an unspoken
agreement that if she becomes incontinent, she will have to go to a nursing
home. I doubt my sister-in-law would actually permit that, but it's the ele-
phant in the room, so to speak, especially for my mother-in-law herself,
since it is the stated reason for why she arranged for her own mother to
go into a home. And I get that. The movie versions of caretaking are easy
to fall for: you wipe their brow; you gently spoon carefully prepared food
into their mouths; you exchange words of love, gratitude, and admiration.
When was the last time you saw an adult being diapered in a feature film?
Now that I think of it, I remember that that German film I told you about

showed the messier side of things, so I guess I should revise that to: the Hollywood version of caretaking.[3]

I remember the first time I saw my father's genitals spilling out from under his hospital gown and the first time I was in charge of giving him a shower. I wanted to be helpful and was grateful that I could be, but it was also awkward to be in that relationship to my own father. It was at least as hard to grasp that he truly couldn't help himself—and I mean that both figuratively and literally. I'm in a very different place with those feelings and situations now because it is so apparent to me that there is very, very little he can do for himself. I believe it's not an exaggeration to say that I feel lucky that sometimes I can help this person who, when he was capable of it, wanted to do so much for me. Still, it's impossible for me not to wonder how I would feel about taking care of Dad if I simply had no time for anything else as a result and no idea when I would get a break.

One of the classic case studies from the early twentieth century on what was then labeled hysteria (and we would now call posttraumatic stress syndrome) concerns a young woman referred to as Irène, who took care of her mother for sixty days without a break. When the mother actually dies, the daughter experiences it traumatically, and she cannot respond appropriately. She laughs at the funeral, insisting that her mother could not be dead because she would have witnessed it, having never left her side while taking such attentive care of her. In the weeks and months that follow, Irène also pantomimes the events of the night of her mother's death in unwilled reenactments. She's institutionalized. Pierre Janet, her doctor, eventually manages to help her through hypnosis and storytelling.[4] One lesson I learned from this case study is that caretaking itself can become as traumatic as any illness.

These thoughts bring me back to a person and a situation from my college and graduate school days. I believe I mentioned Judy to you once before. She was a friend of a friend and about thirty years older than I. She'd been diagnosed with multiple sclerosis just as she was finishing college. The course the disease took in her case was a steady decline. By age thirty she was in a wheelchair, and by age forty she could no longer use her arms. She had some family money that she'd used to set herself up in a lovely home in Cambridge, Massachusetts (not far from my dorm). She had a hospital-style bed and bath added to the first floor and an access ramp built onto the exterior of the house. For personal care, she had some hired helpers, including someone who could load her into and drive her in a van.

Many of Judy's needs were met by a group of young Korean women who had come to the Boston area to study. They lived on the second floor of her home in exchange for caring for her through the night and on the weekends. I never observed any awkwardness on their part about using the lift to put Judy on the toilet or bathing her. To the contrary, they were always very cheerful—as was Judy herself. She led a very active life. She had developed a specialty in tutoring dyslexic children in her home, and she audited literature classes at Boston University. I and many others would read to her: sometimes it would be her assignments, but usually Judy urged me to share the things I myself needed to read for graduate school. Whenever I would call to arrange a time to visit, I would ask her how she was and she would energetically reply: Great! When I'd suggest a meeting time, she'd reply: Perfect! It was one of the most rewarding and inspiring relationships of my life. Wow! Just writing to you about Judy has really perked me up. There's so much more I want to share with you about her and about caretaking, but speaking of what I need to do, I'd better get back to my class prep.

i.

Cornish, NH
January 23, 2012

Dear Irene,

When we were writing about pain, we brought up the idea that the pains we endure in our everyday lives, from minor to significant, can be seen as practice for the time when pain is part of our own dying. In a much broader sense, everything we experience can be practice for a later time when the experience is much more challenging. I'm thinking of this now because I'm some days out from minor surgery to repair an abdominal hernia. Nothing life-threatening, and while I have spent a good deal of time on the couch and had more pain than I or the surgeon expected, it has been a pretty small event, all things considered.

But I have needed a little extra care from my wife, Nora, who has been making all of the meals, checking that I have what I need within reach before she heads out for work or errands, seeing that I take the medication I'm supposed to take when I'm supposed to take it. In a way, we're both getting some practice, although with opposite sides of the caregiving relationship. But it's not a situation that I enjoy. (Except maybe in that little corner of my brain that holds on to the conditioning that males get in our society, a conditioning that makes being taken care of seem natural. I'm not admitting anything, but I probably should be careful not to milk this situation for more than I should.)

Anyway, the discussion you and I are having about caring for a loved one who is approaching death has led me down two different but related paths in the last few days. The first is the way an already-difficult situation might be made even more challenging if the person who is dying and the caregiver do not have the same understanding of what is happening, what the likely outcome is, and what the timing likely will be.

Imagine if you are either very old or very sick, and you see as clear as day that your end is near. You've accepted it. Maybe, depending on what has come before this point, you even welcome it. Now let's say that your primary caregiver is your spouse, or your adult son or daughter, and she or he does not understand or accept what you know in your heart. They can't see the inevitable and do not want you to give in. You can't share what you need to share about your life and its end because the person or people you need to talk with won't hear it. I would imagine that could make communicating, even about routine things, strained.

Imagine it the other way around. You're the caregiver, and you know from what you observe and what doctors and nurses have told you that your husband has little time to live. But he doesn't seem to know that, even though he has been given the same information. He still talks about beating his cancer or getting back on his feet after the stroke. You would love to talk to him about his life and death, to hear what he thinks about both, to maybe ask some questions you've always wanted to ask. But he won't go there, so you can't. How much harder must that make things?

My wife does social work at a nursing home, and she tells me she sees both sides of this often. In her experience, it's more times than not the resident, the elderly person, who sees his or her death in the near future and is more aware of what's going on than the adult child or children. Frequently, Nora tells me, those children are so unable to accept what is happening that they get impatient and frustrated, convinced that Mom or Dad is being stubborn or lazy, when in fact they are just tired. Old and tired, the way we might all expect to be someday, if we think about it.

The second direction my thoughts have taken recently relates to a particularly challenging situation for the caregiver. So now imagine this: You have been in the hospital or nursing home for some days or weeks, recovering from an illness or maybe a fall. Your doctor and your kids want you to go into an assisted-living facility or move into a nursing home. They are convinced that you should not be home on your own. But home is exactly where you want to be. Who should "win"?

I think one of the toughest challenges for someone providing care to a loved one must be accepting that that person has a right to fail. In fact, I suspect that many caregivers never fully accept that. The decision to go home, for instance, even if it is unlikely to work out or last for long, should be made by the person who is sick or dying, unless the medical problems are so significant that being at home is completely unrealistic (although, where that line is drawn is the point, isn't it?). When I say such a person has a right to fail, I should put *fail* in quotes, because even if he is back in rehab or the hospital or the nursing home in a handful of days, it doesn't actually follow that he failed. It might have been just what was necessary for him to get to the point of acceptance that others around him already were at. It might have been that the tie to home was so overwhelming that not going there would have left him feeling that something important had been left undone.

When we talk about the burden of being a caregiver, we usually mean the exhausting aspects of caring for someone's every need. As you wrote in your last note, there are similarities to having a young child, but the direction in which things are heading is opposite, and that makes all the difference. Still, I wonder if the greatest burden isn't trying to walk that fine line between two kinds of caregiving: on the one hand, taking over, being in charge, insisting on how things will be done, and making all the decisions; and on the other, providing what someone needs while allowing him or her the dignity to continue being who he or she is. It can be extra work and worry. It can mean watching someone you love "fail," perhaps even suffer more than you think necessary. It means not looking at the decisions someone makes about how to live at the end of life only in terms of how those decisions affect you, even when they affect you a great deal.

We don't talk about it much—except in jokes about losing our minds someday—but my wife and I are getting to the ages when the odds of something happening to make one of us the caregiver of the other are increasing. I don't know how I'll do in either role when it is something more significant than hernia surgery. I'm fondly attached to my curmudgeonliness, and that doesn't make for a gracious receiver of care, or caregivee. I do know this, though, because we have talked about it: Whichever of us ends up in the role of caregiver, the other will not need to worry about losing self-determination earlier than necessary. Unless, of course, Nora is only saying what she thinks I want to hear, waiting for the chance to take control. Nah.

steve

Lebanon, NH
Saturday, 28 January 2012

Though I did not know you eleven years ago, Steve, somehow it still feels appropriate to be writing to you today in particular. You probably did not realize that yesterday was the eleventh anniversary of the murders of my friends, Susanne and Half Zantop: January 27, 2001. The 27th was a Saturday that year, and ever since, it's actually the last Saturday of the month that weighs me down; so, that's today. You see, in the aftermath of their murders, during the police investigation, and the sentencing hearing—and everything in between—we friends and family learned about and then reenacted in our own minds all the events of that particular day. Each year starting in 2002, I live the last Saturday of January hour by hour, thinking to myself: they're working at their desks; Susanne gets a fax from Pat; now it's time for Susanne to start making lunch; about now the doorbell rings; Half gets up to answer it. I won't go on. I don't want to go on right now. Besides, it's still before noon. But one day before too long, I think I would like to exchange thoughts with you about sudden and violent death. It's something I've thought about a lot. Maybe too much. In any case, it strikes me as bringing up a very different set of challenges—for survivors, anyway, and in my imagination for the dying, too—than the challenges we've been writing to each other about lately, the challenges of life with death for long-term caregivers and those receiving care—caregivees, as you've called them.

I want to pick up on your suggestions about the discrepancies between how caregivers and caregivees might assess their situations. You've mentioned that the individuals in those roles might view quite differently possible recovery or where to do any recovering that can be done. Or, they might not share the same estimate of how close to death the caregivee is. Those differences in turn might lead to inability to talk about certain subjects, whether it's reminiscing, asking for or granting forgiveness, or making funeral plans—and of course a lot of other topics, too. On a practical level, you've raised the issue of where someone goes after a hospital stay. And on both practical and philosophical levels, you've put a positive spin on the idea of failing or, more specifically, letting ill people fail because maybe that's what they need to do in order to change their perceptions of what's going on. Or maybe just because in some scheme of things, we need to let people "be who they are" as long as possible, even if it affects us adversely. I find myself reacting very strongly to your suggestion.

On the one hand, it sounds downright American: individuality is important, and we should let people determine their own lives as much as possible, even if they "fail," even if they suffer more than might be necessary. I gather you also mean: even if they die sooner than they might otherwise, or linger longer. On the other hand, I find my spine stiffening at your suggestion to let someone make decisions that affect other people adversely. That goes against my own ethics, where trying not to hurt someone else is a paramount value.

I've already shared with you some of the consequences of my brother-in-law's decisions around pain medication and the strain those decisions then put on the people he loved the most. An experience I had myself comes close to the scenario you mused about above: After that severe car accident my parents experienced, in which they were both hurt, my father insisted he should be allowed to leave the hospital and go home at the same time my mother was allowed to. But he'd been letting her do a lot of his personal care even in those days. I tried to explain to him that my mother would not be able to help him get dressed because, with her broken sternum, she could barely get her own clothes on. The only thing that was going to help her heal was rest. He insisted to me that he could get dressed by himself. I challenged him on that point, asking him why he'd been letting my mother do it lately if that were true, and he replied: because it's easier. *Of course*, I immediately thought to myself. Out of my mouth shot: "Easier for whom, exactly?" He was silent. Obviously the answer to my question was: easier for him. My pleas to the hospital staff to not release my father only gained us a few days of Mom recuperating at home without him there. When I drove my father back to their house, the first thing he did once inside was to ask my mother to take off his coat. I barked at him, "She can't touch you." He was so surprised, he backed off, and I helped him at that moment and kept watch that he was dressing himself for a few days.

I had to return to New Hampshire, to my husband and to my work, within the week, and I'm sure my parents quickly went back to their old patterns. *Look*, I say to you and to myself: somehow they "got through that," and Mom healed, becoming stronger again, and she's been doing most of his care for the years ever since. I don't know how she has the stamina. To be sure, she does find it. Dad's dementia is so profound now that he has to receive very clear instructions about any moves he makes: "You need to stand now, John"; "Put your feet closer together"; "Push down with your arms"; and so on. As I've already told you, I'm in a very different place myself with regard to helping Dad whenever I can— which is not as often as I wish it were. I'm sharing this old story with you because I think it illustrates that letting someone be himself or herself has serious consequences for others around them—and on some level, we're all dying. Whose self-determination gets to take precedence???

In the case of my mother-in-law, we've watched how with her aging and physical infirmity, she permits herself—I hasten to interject that she is not demented—to say whatever comes into her mind. Often that is hurtful to precisely those who are sacrificing themselves to help her. If a meal isn't exactly to her liking, she'll say so to my sister-in-law who makes sure there are tasty meals and snacks for her mother, all day, every day. Is it really okay that this elderly woman feels no scruples about self-expression? I try to keep my mouth shut. But it's true that when her negative comments are directed my way, I feel hurt even if I don't say anything. And I always feel a sense of outrage when they're directed to my sisters-in-law. I don't know the solution to these dilemmas, but that's the first place my thoughts went when I read your last letter.

Then my thoughts quickly went on to the next thing, and that is to the relations between what I've called primary and secondary caregivers. From sharing thoughts with my sister Maria on these topics, I have learned that it is important not to second-guess the caregiver who is on the ground, so to speak, the person who has to clean, wipe, cook, and clothe caregivees; arrange and execute doctors' appointments; order, organize, and administer medications; and so on. If I've picked up on your train of thought—you are also suggesting that it would be important for those flying into the situation occasionally, whether literally or figuratively, to check in with the primary caretakers about their sense of how close this person is to dying and whether the caregiver and caregivee are on the same page in this respect. In any case, secondary caregivers should try to bring themselves up to speed in terms of what's already happening, rather than coming in and speaking and acting based on their own assumptions about the situation. From my perspective as the individual who is so often coming intermittently into caretaking situations, I would add that it is incredibly helpful when a primary caregiver is able to offer this kind of assessment and give the secondary caregiver assignments. I can attest that ultimately, most of us back-up assistants are simply trying to be helpful, not bossy, and we possibly just need better guidance on how to be so.

Writing to you has distracted me. And that's positive. So, thanks. I hope you're healing quickly and thoroughly. If you're feeling up to it, let's try for a face-to-face conversation soon, okay?

Yours,

Irene

Cornish, NH
February 7, 2012

Dear Irene,

I don't have the association with a particular date, as you do, but I remember well the day the Zantops were killed. I was at my desk in the newsroom, working on the Sunday edition, when a friend from Hanover called me to ask if I knew of anything big going on in her neighborhood. A woman had just come to their door to say something appeared to be terribly wrong at the Zantops' house next door, so my friend's husband and daughter went with the woman (who I later learned is a good friend of yours) and witnessed the horrific scene left behind by the teenage killers. I'm sorry for the grief that is rekindled for you every year at this time.

Your response to my thoughts about caregivers and caregiving was just what I was hoping would come from our exchanges on these topics: two perspectives that might not be all that different in the end, but that stress different priorities reflecting our individual backgrounds and tendencies. I don't see our two views on self-determination as mutually exclusive, if only because what I wrote last time addressed just part of my thinking. For instance, absent dementia, I think it's the responsibility of people who are ill or dying to be gracious and appreciative. I'm not a big fan of people saying whatever is on their mind in the guise of "just being honest," and I don't want to accept it from someone who is dying any more than from someone who is not. I also don't think of that as related to self-determination in the manner of making important decisions about one's own treatment or where one will live, or try to live. It's just bad behavior.

Take the example of your father and his insistence on going home after the car accident, even though you assumed he would, out of life-long habit, overtax your mother. I start from the perspective that anyone in your father's position should have the right to go home even if others think it unwise. But that is too simplistic on its own. There is certainly the consideration that he might be too great a burden on your mother, and it makes sense to advocate in favor of him remaining in the hospital. Physicians, nurses, and social workers could help in evaluating the situation and suggesting what they think should happen. On the other hand, if your mother is capable of deciding, isn't it probably up to her in the end? Even if the rest of the family is against the idea, those two people who have been together for a very long time get to choose their path, together and separately, by which I mean your mother could decide she can't provide what her husband needs, and tell him that. If he insists on coming home anyway, she *could* make clear that she won't be the one taking care of him, leaving him and the family to arrange for other, possibly paid, caregivers. I'm sure that is unlikely in your family, but it's still a choice for her to make and take responsibility for.

The example of your mother-in-law is different. For whatever reason, she has chosen to occasionally be unpleasant to those closest to her. As you've observed, that puts a great strain on the caregivers. But that isn't about self-determination. It's about grace and gratitude, both of which are often pushed aside by fear and by pain. It can take tremendous patience and compassion to be close to that, as well as the occasional willingness to call someone on it. I have talked with caregivers who said calmly to a dying person that they would not accept being mistreated and would not stay in the room while it's going on.

Several years ago, I went through a training program, "Being with Dying," led by the Buddhist teacher Joan Halifax in Santa Fe, New Mexico. (She's the same Joan Halifax who recorded those CDs you borrowed last year.) One message that pervaded lessons throughout the program was this simple one: Everyone is suffering. You are, I am, our loved ones are, and the person being rude to you at a store counter or flipping you off on the highway is. Seen from that view, your mother-in-law's unpleasantness is a result of her suffering. Maybe she's afraid of dying, maybe she is living with regrets, maybe there are things she wants to say but cannot. If one thinks of her as suffering, her rudeness takes on a different cast.

Okay, so that's the ideal I have had in my head for how I might want to respond to a difficult person, one who is dying in bed or being obnoxious behind a retail counter. I've had mixed results in the many "practice sessions" that come up in the course of my daily life. In fact, I decided years ago to no longer simply accept rude service in stores and restaurants. I hope to raise my objections civilly, but I recently snapped rather angrily at a worker in Home Depot for being rude. That did get me another, nicer, salesperson, but I doubt I had a positive impact on the outlook of the first guy.

I'm evolving here as I write. My grandmother was a grouchy, not-easily-satisfied person, especially in her last days. She'd spent many years refining her unhappiness. She lived into her nineties, and I used to say she was living proof that bile is a preservative. I was not involved in her everyday care, but I was exposed to her unpleasantness often enough that I came to believe it made sense to call her on it, even near the end of her life—not with anger, but with a request that she not talk or act that way. It didn't always matter. Once when I was visiting her in the hospital, and she was very uncomfortable, I offered her a little foot massage, which often works wonders to calm someone down. She said okay with a hint of wariness in her voice. I got out my massage oil, placed a chair at the end of the bed and started on one foot. Not ninety seconds in, she barked, "OK, that one's been massaged to death. Do the other one." Ah, well.

So here is where my evolution of thought brings me today: Self-determination is still paramount, in my mind, but that right does not belong solely to the person who is ill or dying. Without an overriding medical reason to keep someone from making the choice he wants to make, such as going home against advice, he should have that opportunity. But everyone around him has the right of self-determination, as well. His wife and children could, with good reason, tell him that he can go home if he wants, but they won't be able to provide the care he needs so he'll have to find some additional help. That might lead him to change his mind, or it might mean his trip home will be a short one.

Just as true, a caregiver such as your sister-in-law has the right to make clear what she will accept from the person she is caring for. I think it was Ann Landers who used to say that nobody can take advantage of you without your permission, and while that's simplistic, there's truth in it.

I know that every individual situation will put pressures on these ideals of mine, and that real life and death don't fit easily into the forms I like to keep in my head. Still, it's helpful for me to think these things through as I watch families in these situations and think of what might happen in my own life. I can think of people close to me who might blow my ideals out of the water if I were in a caregiving relationship with them.

Your story about your parents reminded me of a couple I worked with a few years ago in New Hampshire. My client was a very traditional eighty-plus-year-old Polish man. He was dying, and his wife was handling almost all of his care on her own, exhausting as that was. She didn't seem to resent the fact that he expected that of her. Occasionally in The Hand to Heart Project, I offer short massages to the caregivers of our clients, and one day I told her I'd give her one before giving her husband his session. She got him comfortably in bed to rest while she was on my table. We were only five minutes or so into the massage session when her husband started banging his cane on the floor next to the bed. "I'd better go see what's the matter," she said, and she got off the table. Minutes later, she came back with him, smiling ruefully. When she'd gotten to the room, he had asked: "Is it my turn yet?"

s.

Lebanon, NH
10 February 2012

Dear Steve,

It certainly hasn't always worked out that I get to respond to your interesting reflections immediately, but today we do not have classes at the college because of an outdoor festival referred to as Winter Carnival. So I'm going to grab the chance and write back while most of my reactions to your thoughts are still fresh.

Today is also the day on which Orthodox Christians commemorate Saint Haralambos; all those named after him celebrate their name days on February 10. Name days are a much bigger deal in Greece than are birthdays, and the person celebrating treats his family and friends, rather than the other way around. Haralambos is an important name in my paternal family. My great-grandfather, my paternal grandmother's beloved father, was named Haralambos; my father's brother was named Haralambos in honor of his grandfather; and his grandson, an energetic toddler, carries this name in honor of his grandfather. I'm mentioning this because my Uncle Harry, as we called him, inherited a weak heart from the paternal branch of my paternal family and had major heart surgery in the early days of bypass surgery, when he wasn't yet forty. He had numerous medical procedures in his adult life and alas, he passed away in 2003 at age seventy when he picked up pneumonia during a hospital stay for another condition. I wasn't on the front line of caretaking in that situation, but thinking about Uncle Harry brings into focus how different personalities handle illness, as well as how increasing age and illness can affect the personality one started out with. Heart disease in particular, I believe, can often change someone's character and baseline behavior. I remember I was congratulating him once on his beautiful granddaughters who were visiting from Greece with their father, my uncle's eldest son. The girls were very young at the time, and Uncle Harry responded to my comment by saying that he didn't like the noise of kids anymore and didn't feel any real pleasure from their company. I was shocked to learn this and was very saddened for him. We had been a large gaggle of grand-kids to our grandparents, and they seemed to relish our presence, even when we were rowdy; our uncles and aunts, too, had showered us with attention and affection, including, if not most of all, Harry. Of course, that had been some thirty years prior. The example of my uncle also raises the issue, I believe, of the ill behaving differently with primary caretakers and immediate family versus more distant relatives or just plain other people they come into contact with. To us adult nieces and nephews, for instance, my uncle continued to be a quite jocular, interested, and loving presence pretty much up until he died.

I appreciated very much your analysis of my mother-in-law's misbe-havior with her daughters as possibly due more to suffering or fear, and we can count fear as a kind of suffering. I'm really going to try to wrap my mind and heart around that idea. I am also thinking about a different challenge related to patients' attitudes: it must be very difficult, even painful, for primary caregivers and family members to observe their very grouchy or ungrateful caregivee behaving graciously or charmingly in the presence of non–family members or people they're meeting for the first time. It is usually the case to date, anyway, that my mother-in-law perks up when she sees me and conducts perfectly normal, even energetic conversations. She's a complete charmer when male nurses or aides come to her apartment. Whereas, as I think I've made clear, she often mopes or complains to her daughters.

Yet another related challenge that our exchange is making clearer to me is the fact that the very ill and elderly often don't appear to be "equally" ill or steadily getting weaker. To get back to that crazy situation I mentioned with regard to the aftermath of my parents' car accident, the social workers and nurses *did* assess my father for going to a rehabilitation home. Check this out: in their presence—and we had to take their word for it because no family members were there—he walked forty steps on his own. He's not weak enough to qualify for rehab, they told me. It did me no good to explain that we hadn't seen him take more than ten steps on his own for months prior to the accident! The absurdity of this situation aside, it must be very hard for an exhausted caretaker to hear the caregivee tell the doctor he or she is fine or to observe them perform a task for someone else that they have been letting the caregiver do because they've led her or him to believe they can't do it themselves. While my Dad, for instance, has always been a "performer" for strangers, if I understand the nature of dying and serious illness, it is simply the painful truth that sometimes ill or dying individuals will need help with things one day, and other days they can do perhaps the very same tasks on their own. Furthermore, sometimes they will want to be independent and sometimes they will not.

I'd like to pick up on one additional important point you've made. You suggested that the grumpy elder or even the person cursing you out on the road can be suffering and that if we think of or remind ourselves of that likelihood, it might help us be more gracious and patient with them. If you don't know of it, I recommend to you very highly an extremely short book called *This Is Water*. It's actually the text of a commencement speech given by the writer/philosopher David Foster Wallace at Kenyon College in 2005. It was "rediscovered" and published after his suicide in 2008, and I think it's one of the most beautiful and inspiring pieces of writing I've ever had the privilege to read.[5] His argument goes something like what you've outlined in your previous letter. What if we choose to assume that the person in front of us in the checkout line holding things up, holding ME up—and I'm tired and I want to get home!—has an ill husband and can't make ends meet without using all those coupons? What if we decide to assume that the SUV passing us on our way home and cutting in front of us too rapidly is a desperate father trying to get his kid to the hospital? Will we be able to calm down? Will we be able to send out good vibes instead of angry and annoyed ones? Will we take in any beauty that is around us at that moment? That's the "this is water" part. The book's title comes from an anecdote Wallace relates about an older fish asking younger ones: How's the water today? They're flummoxed because they don't even register that they're swimming in water. In short, the whole point of this little book is about our freedom to make a choice to live with awareness and compassion in the present. While I deeply aspire to the set of attitudes Wallace sketches out, I also know that I can easily get angry or depressed when I see people around me behaving in a hurtful way toward others. You've suggested, as Wallace has, that we could choose to frame what is going on differently: those caregivees behaving badly are doing so because they're scared and hurting, not because they're mean or selfish.

I know that ultimately we can only try to control our own behavior and attitudes. That's why I loved that book and why I love exchanging thoughts with you on these difficult topics.

Yours,

Irene

Cornish, NH
February 17, 2012

Dear Irene,

These letters are like a slowly unfolding conversation, aren't they? Not as slowly as the days when handwritten letters were the typical way of communicating, but sometimes—even with e-mail—more slowly than my impatient mind wants. I find myself forming very specific responses to parts of your notes, wanting to reply in real time. Alas, here is my latest collection of thoughts and responses in what I guess must be unreal time.

You mentioned that it can be tough for someone caring for a loved one who is dying to adjust to how things change from day to day, and not just in terms of the inevitable decline. That is absolutely true. In many cases, dying is not a linear process, with clear and predictable movement in only one direction. One day, even one hour, might be better or worse than the last. There are so many variables in that, too. Medication swings. Comfort/pain levels. Emotional state. The uneven way in which the body lets go of its hold on conscious and unconscious abilities. Routine would be a good thing for a caregiver: knowing what to expect and going about regular tasks to accommodate that. But how do you establish routine when little can be counted on?

What you wrote about caregivees presenting themselves so differently to people other than their family and caregivers also struck a chord with me. The grandmother I mentioned before had that attribute in spades. Many of her friends, and even the nurses and aides in the nursing home where she lived her last couple of years, thought her charming and saw her caustic nature as her own type of humor. Those of us closer to her often saw the caustic without the humor, especially in her last many years. She wasn't happy, and we were the ones who saw that. It was her own suffering, for sure, but it often made having a pleasant conversation with her difficult.

I had another, lighter memory brought up by the story of your dad walking forty steps for the physical therapist but barely ten in front of family. This isn't on quite the same scale, but several years ago I was doing some home-visit massage with a delightful elderly man whose legs had gotten weak and painful. At least once a week for some time, I would show up, and he'd point his walker toward the bedroom, making very slow progress. Once there, I'd help him get his shoes, trousers, and shirt off, then help him get settled on the bed. After the massage, I'd help him back into shirt, pants, and shoes. I don't remember how I got into the habit of helping him in this way, but I do know he happily accepted, even encouraged it. Then, one day, after I'd left his room and was heading toward the door, his wife stopped me and said: "You know, he gets dressed and undressed on his own every day." I'd been scammed.

So much of what we've written in this exchange about caregiving has been about the negative, the challenges that can make it so hard to do, or even to contemplate doing. It's all true, I know, but I want to return to something I mentioned a few letters ago: the gift of being allowed to care for someone. Approaching death is a difficult, messy, and certainly profound experience. It follows, doesn't it, that accompanying someone you love through that experience can be both as difficult and as profound? Life-changing, even. I've talked to many people who've said that no matter how challenging it was, they wouldn't trade the experience of being with their dying parents or siblings or spouses for anything.

Here is a twist on that theme that came to mind recently. Years ago I started giving some in-hospital massage to a man of nearly sixty who was dying of a fast-advancing cancer. He had two daughters in their twenties, and a wife who was with him almost constantly, attending to his needs. A few times, I had the chance to get her into another room on that floor and give her a massage, too, and during one of those sessions she told me what I would never have picked up on otherwise. Her husband had been emotionally abusive for most of their marriage, she said, and she had finally decided to leave him. She'd talked to her pastor and to her daughters, and had contacted an attorney to begin the process. She was about to inform her husband of her decision when he was diagnosed with terminal cancer. She dropped the divorce and became his caregiver.

I know from talking to her that it was something she felt she had to do. I assume she didn't feel the reward one might feel from caring for a husband one truly loves, but I don't think it was an entirely selfless act. The reward she got was from doing the right thing, as she saw it, from being true to her heart and her faith. I've always admired her for that.

Thanks to The Hand to Heart Project, I have been in countless homes in which people were caring for a dying family member or close friend. Each person goes about it differently, but it's not hard to see how tiring, frustrating, scary, and—often—rewarding it is. When I talk to them about it, I always find myself saying pretty much the same thing: "You're doing amazing work." And they are.

s.

IS SUDDEN DEATH DIFFERENT?

Lebanon, NH

23 February 2012

Dear Steve,

So many things on my mind. For starters, though, I'm so pleased we've been able to visit with one another in person and do a different kind of writing—as much as I like this kind. Our upcoming presentation on "Life With Death" to my academic peers at the Narrative Society conference in March is shaping up; I hope you feel sanguine about it, too. I'm so delighted you were game for trying to give our ideas an airing in an academic setting. I'm curious how we will be received. But I also like the idea of us continuing with these private exchanges. I feel "uncensored" in this conversational space we've created by writing to each other over e-mail. It gives me a chance to try out ideas and express feelings—not always admirable ones—on the most difficult subjects, and that's been clarifying for me, if not life-changing.

Having said that clears the way to another of the things on my mind. Today I participated in a panel discussion at the college called "Professing Our Deepest Convictions." I agreed to participate because I wanted to challenge myself to see if I in fact could articulate my deepest convictions. It was a tough assignment. I'm mentioning it to you here because as I prepared my remarks, I realized more clearly than I ever have before how much I have been marked, I believe almost formed, by the experience of having lost my friends, Susanne and Half, to violent death. Of course those deaths are a hidden thread in my relationship to you, too. Having promised you repeatedly that I would like to share some thoughts about the Zantops' murders, I realized today that maybe it was time I made good on this.

You know something of the facts, of course, being a member of the small community where these violent deaths occurred, and I know you've read my book *Daddy's War*, where I discuss how my experience of the Zantops' murders pushed me to try to learn more about the traumas in my own family closet. I wrote about losing the Zantops also one other time, in the national and international contexts of 9/11.[1]

Those opportunities to try to process the experience through writing about it were crucial to me and my mental health. What I was thinking about in preparation for today's discussion on "Professing Our Deepest Convictions" is the paramount value I put on kindness. I'm the first to admit that I'm not always kind. Still, I professed publicly at school today that while I don't have that many deeply held convictions, trying to be kind is definitely one of them. I think that's what's behind some of my distressed reactions in our recent exchanges on caregiving, when I reported on ill people I knew who were not being nice to their caregivers—or when I myself was not being very kind in my judgmental attitude toward them!

You might well be asking what kindness has to do with murder. Acts of kindness and acts of killing do seem so completely alien to one another, after all. Well, actually kindness enters into my experiences in a number of different ways.

In the first instance, when the details came out about what actually transpired in the Zantops' home the day they were killed, a number of them reflected Susanne and Half's deep commitment to kindness, even kindness to strangers. A kindness I can only label as the most true Christian kindness, though Susanne and Half would not have thought of it that way themselves—for me another proof of its Christian nature. Half not only opened the door to two unknown teenagers in the first place, he brought them into the couple's study and tried to answer their questions (they claimed to be conducting a survey). When he found their questions not pertinent or well organized enough, he took out his wallet to find the telephone number of someone he thought they should talk to in order to improve their project. It seems that the view of the wallet and its contents reminded the teenagers that they were in search of notoriety, and that's when they pulled out their knives.

I don't intend to take you or me through the series of fatal events that transpired next. But to stick with "kindness," I will tell you that the autopsies revealed defensive cut marks on the back of Half's hands. So, you see, he didn't strike out; he only tried to protect himself. He must have cried out, though, because that appears to be when Susanne came rushing into the study from the kitchen where she'd been preparing lunch. That desire to help Half sealed her fate, as Half's willingness to help the boys sealed his.

In the aftermath of learning such details, I found myself repeatedly trying to "walk through" the last moments of my friends' lives. I did so by visualizing that four human beings were in very close physical contact, and two of those humans used sharpened steel on the flesh of the other two. This struck me at the time—and still does—as quite different from killing by shooting with a gun. There's not only usually more distance with a firearm, but the physical action of pulling a trigger is quite different—and rather innocuous, don't you think?—from a physical motion that inflicts pain on another human being with a knife or bludgeon. Stabbing or strangling or other methods that bring murderer and victim into direct physical contact is the opposite of kindness, if I might phrase it that way to stick with my theme. I worried deeply about what it must have felt like to my friends to be on the receiving end of this "opposite of kindness." Many trauma specialists report that violence that is man-made (like murder, rape, personal attacks) has more virulent effects on survivors than does violence that comes from nature (like earthquakes, tsunami, etc.)[2]—though of course myriad factors can affect the development and course of posttraumatic stress disorder. Alas, Susanne and Half didn't survive. Did they have a chance to process what was happening to them? Let me try that again: Do you think that when death comes that quickly people still have a moment to register it? Do they experience the proverbial "your whole life flashes before your eyes," I wonder? The friend who discovered their dead bodies said that Half had a peaceful expression on his face. That thought has comforted me many times. It also intrigues and challenges me. Is there anything we humans can do to try to enhance the chances that our last earthly moment will be peaceful, no matter how it was precipitated?

Having experienced the death of my brother-in-law recently and of course in the more distant past of other individuals I have loved deeply, such as my friend Judy or my Uncle Harry, about whom I've written you, I believe that mourning in the wake of a violent death is quite different. Certainly it has been for me. The very unexpectedness of learning the Zantops had been killed caused first a profound disbelief and then a profound numbing. I think the reaction of disbelief is understandable: What? Here? In this peaceful town? Kill these gentle and loving people? My precious friends and mentors, dead?

The numbing was more surprising to me than the disbelief, in part because it or maybe the recognition of it physically pained me. In the immediate days following the murders, hours would go by without me registering the passing of time at all. When I would "come to," I ached all over, as if a professional boxer had just had her way with me. Then there were the moments of sheer terror when I would be looking at the person I was with and be overwhelmed with the absolute conviction that he or she was going to die soon. That terror felt like stabs with a really sharp knife. For months and months (even years, though mercifully occurring less and less frequently), there were also sudden torrents of tears. My inner being rarely gave me any warning for these crying episodes, so I could not prepare for becoming dysfunctional. It's not just the eyes that hurt when you cry that hard, it's the chest, too. There was one other emotion that invaded my inner being in that period, one that I am particularly embarrassed about. I guess I would have to describe it as a refusal to go on. In my case, this took the particular form of not wanting to assume professional or departmental responsibilities that would come to me now that Susanne was gone (we were teaching in the same department and programs, and she was chairing our home department of German Studies at the time of her death). This weird "refusal" had its physical component, too; it was as if my inner attitude could be read on my face like a blush, and I was trying to do everything to prevent it from showing. What I was internally experiencing as my immaturity extended to my not wanting to make decisions about my own life because I couldn't consult with Susanne and Half, who had been my mentors and confidantes for years with regard to almost any major issue that came up for me.

So, here's where kindness, though of a different type, applies to my experience. I had to learn to not judge my grieving self; to accept that I was going to feel strong emotions that I would normally judge as ugly and undesirable. I should not try to suppress those emotions if I wanted the mourning to find its end. In short, I had to be kind to myself. That took a lot of will power: I had to consciously stop certain trains of thought, but do so in a gentle, merciful manner.

There's a lot more I could share, but I've shed buckets of tears trying to write even this much to you and I'm exhausted.

Thanks for listening in a kindly way, as I know you will.

i.

P.S. Thanks for the *Handbook for Mortals* volume. Not quite sure when I'll get to it, but it looks like it'll be really useful. I like the clear layout and the inclusion of questions one could pose to one's doctors.

Cornish, NH
February 28, 2012

Dear Irene,

Whenever we have talked about the Zantops' murders, and certainly when I read that section of your book *Daddy's War*, I feel I have understood the depth of your pain. It is horrible to know two people so intimately, to love them so much, and hold that in your mind alongside what you know about the way they died. I know that when I hear or read about such a violent death, one that must have been horrible to endure, I immediately begin thinking: It's over. However awful it was at the time, it's over. And whatever, if anything, comes after this life, for those people death brought an end to that particular suffering.

You ask a fascinating question about their deaths, and about the deaths of people who come to their ends suddenly, with or without violence. (I understand that about one in ten of us will die that way.) Do people who die suddenly have even a millisecond of awareness that they're dying? Do they have even the briefest of chances to process what is happening, and to perhaps prepare themselves?

It's an odd thing to wonder, in a way. Can anything meaningful happen in a few seconds, or in a fraction of a second? Maybe it is, as you suggest, a variation on the notion of one's life passing before one's eyes in almost no time. In this case, perhaps it's not the events of your life, but the meaning of it and of your death—and your sense of what is to come after this life, if anything. All in a few minutes, or seconds, or less.

I wonder if one can perhaps prepare even for a very sudden death. I don't mean prepare by leading an exemplary life and being ready to meet one's maker in good spiritual standing. I mean be ready for the event itself, prepared in a way that permits a sudden, and even violent, death to be as meaningful in its way as one that comes after a long illness with time to set affairs in order.

We both know the stories told about the death of Mahatma Gandhi in

1948. (I also mentioned it to you in one of our earlier exchanges.) He was shot at close range while walking through a crowd on his way to a meeting. There are varying accounts of what he said as he fell to the ground with three bullet wounds in his chest and stomach. Apparently, it was either "Hey Ram," translated as "Oh God," or "Rama, Rama," or maybe "Ram, Ram." Ram, or Rama, is a Hindu deity, and since Gandhi had said in a speech months before that even if he was killed—there had been several unsuccessful attempts on his life—he would not give up invoking the name of God, it seems reasonable to assume that in the split second he had after the shots were fired, he went immediately to a place of comfort and peace, the place he wanted to be when he died, whenever and however that happened.

Gandhi might not seem the best example, because he knew he was targeted by his enemies and that he could die at any moment. But isn't that just another way of experiencing what is true for all of us? We can all be as sure as Gandhi was that we will die someday, maybe soon. And we could all aspire to being so prepared for the end of this life that when it comes, whether in the snap of fingers or more gradually, we have our version of "Ram, Ram" on our lips.

But how to do that? This is the heart of what our exchange of letters is about, I think.

Accepting my mortality doesn't mean accepting that I will die someday in a comfortable bed with my loved ones close by and with plenty of opportunity to make peace with my God or gods, and with my demons (definitely more than one of those). In fact, I sometimes think that in these discussions of ours, and in the talks I've had with clients and others, I can feel myself getting a little cavalier about dying. A little too comfortable with how I've figured it all out. In his book *The Tibetan Book of Living and Dying*, Sogyal Rinpoche addressed this idea when he wrote about coming to the West and being surprised at peoples' attitudes toward death. Many, he observed, live "either in denial of death or in terror of it. . . . Many people believe that simply mentioning death is to risk wishing it about ourselves."[3]

Others—and this is where I wonder if he was thinking about me—"look on death with a naïve, thoughtless cheerfulness, thinking that for some unknown reason, death will work out all right for them, and there is nothing to worry about. When I think of them, I am reminded of what one Tibetan master says: People often make the mistake of being frivolous about death and think, 'Oh, well, death happens to everybody. It's not a big deal. I'll be fine.' That's a nice theory until one is dying."[4]

Accepting my mortality has to mean knowing that death could come in a way far different from the peaceful deathbed image in my imagination, including that I could have a heart attack today and be gone, period. Or a car accident. Or that someone with my death on his mind could knock at my door.

I don't want to just "know" that that is true and then carry on. I want what flashes before my eyes, if anything does, to be . . . Okay, I'm at a loss to say what I want.

This Las Vegas trip to read our paper at the Narrative Society meeting, by the way, is a fascinating prospect for me. That's not a city I have longed to visit, and I certainly never expected to be presenting a paper at a meeting of an international academic organization. I have no idea what to expect. I'm wide open to whatever happens, although I wonder if that's a good way to approach a visit to Vegas.

s.

Lebanon, NH
2 March 2012

Dear Steve,

Did I ever share that Gandhi is one of my earliest and most consistently admired heroes? I read tons about him and by him when I was a kid. My adult self realizes that not everything he did was heroic and that not all concerned parties were in agreement about the specific path to independence for India he endorsed, but that doesn't prevent me from admiring how thoroughly he lived his beliefs, even when nonviolence was inconvenient or unpopular. The anecdote about his last words fits what I've always admired about him. I particularly like the way you expressed how in that final conscious moment, however brief it might have been, he seems to have managed to get himself to the place he wanted to be at the end of life. That mental place was, as I understand it, not hating the killer, but peacefully nestling close to his god. When you talk about how to have our own version of "Rama, Rama" on our lips, I think about two things: what images and memories would I choose to have in mind during my last minutes, and what words would I choose to have coming out of my mouth? For any chance of either or both of those to happen—especially with a sudden or unexpected death—it seems likely to me that one would have to think about it, choose, and practice beforehand.

You probably know that last words have been important to many Christians as a reflection of St. Paul's injunction to pray without ceasing (1 Thess. 5:17). If one indeed prays constantly, then one will obviously be praying at one's human end. Many Christians, especially in Eastern Orthodoxy, use the Jesus Prayer ("Lord Jesus Christ, Son of God, have mercy on me, a sinner") as a path to this ideal of praying always. The Jesus Prayer is also referred to as the prayer of the heart, and recital of it in the strictest practices is linked to deep breathing and even the beating of the heart. Monks are warned by their elders about its power, almost like warning about taking too strong a dose of a drug. Even for us amateur practitioners, invoking the Holy Name of Jesus has particular power and thus one would want to always have it on one's lips.

To me, thinking and practicing "last words" well before you suspect your last breath is actually near is ultimately a decision about expressing verbally the essence of your life, not an obsessive preparation for your death. I guess that's why I, too, practice the Jesus prayer. For me, God truly is love, and so to die with Jesus's name on my lips would be to try one more time actively to be in a state of loving—forgive the oxymoron. Closely linked to that is my ideal to feel only gratitude for the beauty of life and God's gifts at the end of my mortal existence. So naturally I try to practice feeling grateful and to call up images and memories for which I am grateful, like beautiful places I've been, the sweet faces and smiles of people I've loved, moments of feeling in harmony and peace with others.

Another way I've thought of this, especially in the wake of the Zantops' murders, is: if this will be my last moment—and it very well could be since none of us knows when our moment of death will arrive—how do I want to be living it? This was another way in which kindness entered into that stage of grieving in my life, to continue that theme from my previous letter. If I found myself thinking mean or dissatisfied thoughts, I would often jar myself out of them by reminding myself that if this is my last or next-to-last moment on Earth, that's not the way I want to be feeling.

Recently I found myself thinking about Jesus's human death in that context. He himself chose to get to the place he wanted to be by focusing not on his pain but on the act of granting forgiveness: "Forgive them, Father, for they know not what they do" (Luke 23:34).

Thinking about sudden death brought to mind something much more secular I read last summer. I think I told you about me stumbling across a book called *vous parler de la mort*.[5] The title's not that easy to translate, but it means something like: "to talk to you about death" or "talking to you about death." The book was published in 2003, and the author is a man named Bernard Crettaz, who is a Swiss from the canton Valais. It's the area to the east of where my husband is from; it's literally a very deep, wide, long valley with high mountain valleys off of it. The bigger valley runs approximately east–west, and the smaller ones north–south. Some of the most visited places in Switzerland are there, like Zermatt and the Matterhorn, known in French as the Cervin. The exact place Crettaz is from is called Val d'Anniviers. It's in a valley slightly to the west of the one that Zermatt helps form. I'm not sure about the earlier history of the place, but it became rather well known when an anthropologist, Yvonne Preiswerk (who had met and become the spouse of Crettaz), published a book about Val d'Anniviers, particularly about its mortuary customs. I've read that book, too, *Le Repas de la mort* [The Meal of Death] (published in 1983).[6]

If you don't mind my telling you a bit about him, you'll see that I'll get back to our topic of sudden death. Crettaz was born in 1938 and studied theology and sociology. His main jobs were running the European section of the Ethnological Museum in Geneva and teaching sociology at the University of Geneva. He's probably best known for three things. First, he founded the Society for Thanatological Studies (from the Greek word for death, *thanatos*). Second, he helped conceive and mount a major exhibition about death, "La mort à vivre." This is very hard to translate, too; the phrase *à vivre* is the same in French as English, when you say: he has two months *to live*. So the phrase is striking, but somehow recognizable; it could be translated something like: "to live death," or "experiencing death." Another echo in the French title is the idea of doing something—*à faire*—so that strain could be translated as something like "to do death," maybe even "to go forward with death." The exhibition provided copious information on how different cultures around the world deal with death in the sense of funeral rites, mourning rituals, and so forth, but it was also designed to help people concretely start to think about how they might themselves go through mourning the death of a loved one. It ran from October 1999 to April 2000 at the Ethnological Museum in Geneva.[7]

The third thing Crettaz became known or notorious for was a *Café mortel*, a meeting that was specifically designed for people to come and discuss thoughts about dying, death, and mourning. The *café* part has to do with literally holding the discussion (and subsequent ones) in local cafés. Utilizing the space and ambiance of cafés reflects Crettaz's conviction that mortality is a topic like many others; we shouldn't banish death from our everyday world of interactions. Since 2003, Crettaz has been fully retired from teaching and working at the museum, has returned to his home area, and he dedicates himself to writing. He's written or cowritten about a dozen books by now, including one on the Cafés mortels.[8]

Yvonne, in contrast, died relatively young, quickly, and unexpectedly. Bernard had dropped her off at the hospital for routine medical exams in April 1999, during the period in which they, with others, were preparing the big exposition on death for the museum I already mentioned. While Yvonne was undergoing a test to check her heart function, her heart stopped. The staff revived her artificially, but she never came back to consciousness. Bernard was called and had to decide what to do. He was completely shocked by the situation, though he and Yvonne had spent much of their adult lives studying death. In a number of interviews with him I've read, and also in the little book I started telling you about, he describes how he retreated to a side room and convoked his dead; that is, he tried to bring to mind his ancestors and all the people he'd known who had died, summoning them to consult with them about what he should do. He reports that having heard from them, he was then able to return to Yvonne's room and ask the staff to stop the artificial respiration. She subsequently died.

There are other interesting and telling details about how Bernard processed Yvonne's death, the most compelling to my mind being his own admission that he was completely unprepared for it. What's so remarkable about that? you might well ask. But then I'd remind you, we're talking about two people who spent their professional lives studying death and death rituals. That's why it particularly fascinated me that Bernard didn't know what Yvonne's wishes were concerning some basic issues like whether to be buried or cremated, what kind of funeral service or mourning rituals to follow, and so on. He felt guilty that he didn't know what she would have wanted, until someone in his circle of friends urged him that he shouldn't worry about that because it's the living who get to decide what to do with the dead.[9]

I was struck by the pastor who told him that he needed to leave the religious service to her, and that his job was to focus on experiencing it, on living it. He comments that he felt "liberated" once she'd said this to him.

In mentioning how unprepared he was for his wife's death, Crettaz generalizes from his own experience to suggest that we are never prepared for death, regardless of whether we're "death professionals" or nonprofessionals, religious or nonreligious people. Another way he puts it is that we cannot be sure how we are going to react to the death of loved ones. This last accords with the advice I was given by mental-health professionals when we were preparing for my father's open heart surgery almost fifteen years ago. I was advised to try not to predetermine how I might react to my father's death or to try to control my grieving if he did die. I didn't lose my father in that surgery, thank God, especially since he had a few really good years after that. This same advice, though, helped me a lot when we lost the Zantops.

One other thing that struck me about Crettaz's report about losing his wife so suddenly was his discovery of how important having a community is. He states several times that mourners need people around them, specifically mentioning that they have a great need for others to listen to them, even long after the death of their loved ones has occurred. I know that when I was in the more active phase of mourning the Zantops—it's never completely over, I think—it was like a dividing line, like a separating of the proverbial sheep and goats. Unwilled, I automatically noted who was too afraid to be near me because I might talk about the Zantops, and who made me feel pretty sure that it was okay to be who I was, which was a person actively grieving them.

This week I was lucky enough to see two of my beloved friends who were themselves extremely close to the Zantops. We always just pop back into being comfortable with one another even if it's been a while since our last visit. I often think of that as Susanne and Half's legacy to us, cultivating such a loving and loyal community of friends. Building and simply enjoying "community" were top priorities for Susanne. She never liked to be away from the Hanover area for too long because she missed her "community." It was funny, because even when she was speaking in German, she would say that word in English.

So, with the precious sound of Susanne's voice in my head, I'll sign off. *See* you, soon, though!

i.

Cornish, NH
March 19, 2012

Dear Irene,

So, now I can say that I have been to Las Vegas. And just as surely, I can say that I don't need to go back. For all of its indulgences in extremes of human behavior, I found it one of the least life-affirming places I have been to. The conference, though, was pretty fascinating to me. I also thought the paper we delivered was a clear and intriguing collaboration on our parts, a great boiling down of some of what we've been writing recently.

And now, back to that.

One concept of Eastern thinking that I particularly like—and I'm no scholar of the traditions, so this will be a great oversimplification—is the importance of being able to hold two seemingly opposite truths in our minds at once, and accept both. In some traditions, an example would be the truth that I am here, alive in this world, typing at this moment on my laptop, sitting in my living room, which has a sofa and woodstove and television; while alongside that would be the truth that none of those things actually exist, and that my physical self and everything around me are illusions—a lot of individual illusions that are causally, or at least temporally, related. It takes some effort, practice, in fact, to make those two truths sit comfortably in the same mind.

I'm thinking of that concept right now because of what might seem to be contradictory truths in what we have been writing in these letters. We have been telling ourselves that we can prepare for our own deaths and the deaths of those around us by contemplating the truth of mortality, and accepting it; that we can even change our lives by thinking about death and preparing for it. The change might be as simple as a recognition of the fact of mortality; its proximity makes us realize that our lives are comparatively short and we should make the most of this life that we have and value the moments we have with the ones with whom we share it. It could end in a heartbeat, so every heartbeat is an incalculable treasure.

Anyway, along comes Bernard Crettaz, a "death expert" if ever there was one, who was apparently as unprepared as anyone else might be for the sudden death of his wife. His conclusion was that we are never truly prepared for death.

Can we be right if he is? Can both of these perspectives be true? I hope so, because I suspect there is no denying what Crettaz says. With the possible exception of monks and others like them who live isolated and contemplative lives, we spend our days immersed in a busy world, which includes taking for granted the people, the very scenery, around us. Even if we've spent months or years thinking about our mortality (or exchanging e-mails on the topic), how can it not be a shock when death or life-threatening illness breaks into that routine? When somebody is suddenly gone?

It seems clear that when a particular, sudden death happens in our lives, how we react and how prepared we are (if at all) will depend on where we are in our own life journeys at that moment. How many deaths have we experienced by that time, and under what circumstances? Old age? War? Accidents? What did we learn of death in childhood or young adulthood?

I've spent a lot of time thinking about mortality over the last many years, as I've worked with people who are ill or dying. If someone close to me died suddenly now, I would probably be as unprepared as Crettaz was, but perhaps prepared enough to make sense of things, to regain my equilibrium, before too long. In 1983, when I was twenty-seven, though, I might have been the very picture of unprepared. The word *clueless* comes to mind. That is how old I was when my father died of a heart attack. He was fifty-five, which didn't seem nearly as young at the time as it does now, not surprisingly.

I had started a new job as an editor at the *Valley News* in your town, Lebanon, New Hampshire, only a few months before—the first in a series of positions that would eventually lead to our meeting. At the outset I was generally pretty nervous. Nervous about fitting in, nervous about making mistakes, especially mistakes that didn't get caught until after the press rolled. I was nervous about handling the workload and not seeming as though I was in over my head, which I was for a while. Late one night, the phone rang at home, and it was my brother telling me that Dad had had a heart attack. He was in the hospital, but they thought he was out of the woods.

I was stunned. Dad and I had had an up-and-down relationship for some years, but I thought of us as close, and I don't think I had ever considered the possibility that he would die before reaching a ripe old age. I didn't know enough to see the extra weight he carried for many years, the cigarette smoking that led to violent coughing fits in the mornings, and the heaping platefuls of food he ate at dinnertime as combining to become a threat to his longevity.

I was stunned, as I say, which isn't an excuse for the foolish mistake I made next. I told my brother I'd be there as soon as I could, and then I went in to the office early to jam my way through as much of my day's work as I could so nobody else would be inconvenienced. When I had gotten through what I thought would be enough, about midmorning, I headed out. The hospital was a two-hour drive away. When I arrived, my mother and sister were tearfully walking from my father's room to a sitting room. He had just died. For the sake of keeping anyone at work from having to cover for me, I'd missed being with Dad in his last hours.

It took me a long time to stop beating myself up over that one. I wish now that, at the age of twenty-seven, I had done the thinking and reading on end of life and mortality that I've done since, but how many twenty-somethings in our culture do that?

And I wonder, as I look back on that day thirty years ago, what Dad's experience was. Was he afraid? Was he caught entirely by surprise? Did he think about me, my brother, and my sisters? Did his mind go to the parts of his life that were really hard and painful, or to happier times? Was he able to see his death coming and make some peace with the idea?

When people have a predicted approach to their deaths, they

often worry a great deal about unfinished business, about relationships unmended, about mundane and important tasks uncompleted. And from what I've seen, when the end gets very close, those worries, so grounded in this life, frequently become much less important. Can that transition also happen in a second, or a minute? I wish I knew whether my father experienced any such shift in his very brief time between heart attack and death.

The last conversation I had had with him, by phone, was an uncomfortable one. My wife and I, married for less than a year, had invited family over for a cookout just days earlier, and Dad wasn't impressed with my abilities as a host. He was critical of how we had done things, and I was probably a little defensive. But it ended well. We talked it out, I told him I loved him, and he said he loved me. Having that memory has made a great difference to me, considering the less-pleasant ones I have regarding his death. Thank heavens for that.

S.

P.S. Crettaz's Café mortel idea is intriguing. I'd like to see us consider putting together something like that for ourselves around here.

Lebanon, NH
25 March 2012

Dear Steve,

I'm still reeling, in a good way, from presenting the paper with you and being on the panel dedicated to "The Dying and the Living" at the narrative conference. It was so meaningful and helpful to me to be thinking about these issues in a professional context, in that room, with those people present. We didn't have a big audience, but several of the individuals who attended our talk and certainly the other folks on the panel were people I admire, people whose ideas I care to hear. I felt in a way like that presentation allowed events I'd been experiencing very intensely in my personal life to be sewn together with thoughts you and I have been exchanging in this protected space of written exchanges, and to be sewn together with my decades-long professional preoccupations with literature and a certain way of presenting ideas. In other words, three very different arenas of my life were brought into dialogue with each other by focusing on this topic. That felt very affirming. Thank you again for being such a good sport about it and giving "my world" a try. Thank you, too, for continuing so quickly the thread of this, our private exchange. Finally, for now, anyway, thank you for sharing about your father.

I knew that family relations, that is, with your nuclear family, have been strained at times, but I didn't know about that particular piece of it. Reading what you wrote made it sound to me like ultimately you have come to understand a lot about how and why you "missed" your father's death. I suspect that that experience may have conditioned your choices around other unexpected pieces of news in its aftermath, and I hope that is a comfort.

I was mightily helped by my mother in a somewhat-similar situation with the passing of a beloved relative in Greece. I had recently completed my doctorate and was teaching at the University of Texas at the time. I knew that my Uncle Takis—I called him uncle, but he was technically my maternal grandmother's first cousin—had been diagnosed with lung cancer. The news had made me very sad, but it wasn't shocking, given what a lifelong heavy smoker he was. I had been planning to visit him in the following summer; it would be my first vacation in ages, free from the weight of an unfinished dissertation. My mother called me one winter evening, though, and said: "Irene, Takis is in the hospital. If you want to see him, you'd better go now." And I did. I dropped everything immediately. I had colleagues cover my classes. I paid a fortune for the plane ticket. And I flew to Greece in the middle of the first Gulf War. (At least the plane was empty from a general fear of flying and I could stretch out.) Other relatives, one of my mother's sisters and her husband, met me at the Athens airport and took me straight to the hospital. Takis had been told I was on the way, and though he seemed weak, he responded to my arrival coherently. I poured out all the greetings I was bringing from the family in the United States, profusely and repeatedly saying thank you and expressing how much I loved him. He was his characteristic self, that is to say, he was selfless, and he wondered where I would sleep that night, as I always stayed with him when I was in Athens. When he was satisfied that I'd be taken care of, we said good night and I headed to my mother's sister's place. I finally got some rest. First thing in the morning, we, my aunt and her husband, along with Takis's only brother and his wife, headed straight back to the hospital. I was the youngest and fastest member of the group and raced ahead of them. What a shock I got to turn the corner into his hospital room and see an empty, freshly made-up bed where just a few hours prior my beloved uncle had lain. It was like having the wind knocked out of me.[10] Still, I had done what I knew I wanted to do, and I felt deeply grateful that I had been able to say thank you and good-bye to him before he died.

Takis was an amazingly grounded individual who always thought about helping others. I feel so lucky to have known him. I think the fact that I knew how I felt about him had helped me all along to "not delay"; I don't just mean not delay getting on a plane when my mother suggested I do so, but also not delay in telling him how much he meant to me. I'm pretty sure he felt as cherished by me as I felt cherished by him during the whole course of our relationship. When we went to his apartment later on the day of his death, in the pile of his uncollected mail in the foyer, there was a letter from me that contained pages from my doctoral dissertation, specifically, the acknowledgments, with a message from me to him in Greek explaining that he was named in those pages and thanking him again for all the support he'd given me over the years by believing in me and my talents. I'd sent that letter before I learned how close he was to his death.

I see I've used the word *luck* in telling you about this. I believe lots of things we want or hope for ourselves are not directly attributable to our own actions. Does it help to say that I had good luck in getting to my uncle in time and you had bad luck in not getting to your father in time to say good-bye? Help what? you might well ask. Well, I guess, help us to deal with what comes afterward. I do think my mourning of Takis was eased along by knowing I'd done what I could to express what I had in my heart. I hope I would have felt that way even if he had died while I was en route. Of course I would have been sad not to have managed to see him and tell him one more time how much I loved him and how grateful I was for all he'd done for me. I guess the main lesson to be learned here is the value of trying to live our relationships honestly and fully at all moments, not just the big ones, because you might miss those through no fault of your own. Or maybe it's even more helpful to think about all moments as the big moments. Let me try this one more time: maybe all moments when we are really tuned in to what matters are the big moments. That's one of my definitions of paradise: being completely tuned in to the present.

I'm thinking of that formulation because this discussion brings to mind a moment when I myself almost died. In that same period of teaching in Texas when I lost my uncle, I didn't own a car and went almost everywhere by bike. One night I'd worked late in my office, then gone to hear some music with friends, and then, despite their offer to drive me home later, took off on my bike so I could do some more work at home before turning in. I was in a great mood and enjoying the ride after a fun evening. At a familiar intersection not too far from my apartment, I stopped at a red light and then pushed on when I was sure it was about to turn green. In the middle of the intersection, I noticed car headlights coming at me from my left. I found myself incredibly calmly posing the question: "Oh, what's that car doing there?" Then there's a hole in my memory—I don't remember being hit at all. It wasn't until I was under the car and realized that I was looking at the back side of the front license plate that I realized I was physically trapped under both the car and my bike and started to panic. I'm not sure the rest of the details are that relevant to our discussion, except that, like with any kind of falling, I suspect I'd injured myself less because I was completely relaxed at the moment of impact. I'm not sure I could have programmed myself in advance to be calm in such a scenario. Rather, I'm wondering if it wasn't more for the fact that in the moments prior, I was so happily registering the beauty of the night, the great feeling of physically propelling myself forward, thinking how I loved my life, thankful that I loved life.

Since we started this thread in our correspondence, I find myself returning over and over to your vision of Gandhi's final moments, with him instantaneously getting himself to the place he wanted to be in when he died, to a place of peace and comfort, nestled up to his god or at least in communion with him. I wonder if that isn't how my friend Half managed to die with a peaceful countenance. The bullet, the knife, the car are unstoppably about to arrive, are arriving, and we make the decision to locate ourselves in the place we always want to be. Is that life with death, do you think?

i.

Cornish, NH
April 2, 2012

Dear Irene,

When is a place not a place? We're using a word that normally applies to a physical location to refer instead to a state of mind, possibly a state of soul. Yet it is just the right word. Often, when I have a massage client on my table, if things are going particularly well, he or she will drift off a bit. Not asleep and not awake. Present, but not entirely in the room. In a different place; in the interstitial spaces of consciousness.

The more often or regularly someone gets massage, I find, the more easily and quickly they slip into that place. What you and I are suggesting is that the same can be true in the very different context of the end of life. That it, too, requires the practice of frequently going there, so that the last going might be more comfortable than it might have been otherwise. Remember that passage from the Montaigne essay I cited a while back, that to rob death of its power over us, we should think about it often, get comfortable with it, "wait for it everywhere"?

And yes, I do think that that practice, that familiarity with a place of spiritual comfort and peace, is one of the things we have meant by the notion of life with death.

So, before we leave the topic of sudden death, I wanted to share a couple of the ways my mind has wandered with the topic. We have mostly considered the suddenness of death from the dying person's perspective—that is, it was sudden and unexpected for that person. It's also a sudden death for those who knew him or her, but from that viewpoint, even a death that's a long time coming can be sudden. How often have you found out that someone you knew had died after a long illness when you'd had no idea the person was ill? It's a sudden event for you, in that case. I know it's not the same as the types of deaths we've been discussing here, but I have been hit hard many times by learning of the death of someone I cared for but wasn't in touch with.

And then there is suicide. A very sudden end, but perhaps also one that is a long time coming. (I'm not thinking here about people nearing death and deciding to end their life "early" and on their own terms.) It's so hard for me to imagine the desperation that such an act must come from, and I guess that's because of both the suddenness and the finality of it. A long time ago, I wrote an article about repeat drunken drivers, trying to get at why they do it. In part, I focused on a man who had a long history of such offenses and was no longer supposed to be driving. One evening, he crashed head-on into another car, killing two people. When police and emergency personnel arrived, they looked at him in his car, saw he was alive, and then ran to see to the others. The man reached under the seat of his car, pulled out a handgun that I can easily imagine he kept there for just this purpose, and killed himself.

Three sudden and senseless deaths, but for some reason, the one that has stuck with me is the drunken driver's. I'm thinking of what we wrote earlier, that everyone is suffering. His suffering must have been immense. When I was writing that article, I interviewed a psychologist who specialized in alcohol and substance abuse and who understood such suffering. When I told him how the driver had died, his reaction was not the one many other people would have had—that the man deserved to die, or that he died because of terrible choices he had made over many years. Rather, it was almost shockingly compassionate. He said: "That poor guy." I have wondered if the man had prepared himself in his own way, maybe knew that that was how he would likely die his sudden death, and even had practiced for his death in his mind as his way to achieve peace. A sad thought, I know.

S.

CHAPTER 6

WHAT COMES AFTER I DIE?

Cornish, NH
April 12, 2012

Dear Irene,

It's early gardening time in this part of the world, when people are shedding winter like a snake's skin and heading to the dirt. Many will have their peas and maybe some greens planted before long, if they haven't already. This time of year often makes me think of my neighbor Dora, who lived across the road with her daughter, Sandy, and who loved few things more than puttering in her gardens in spring and in summer, often barefoot.

This is also around the time of year when Dora died. She'd been diagnosed with cancer some eighteen months earlier and was told she might have as little as three months to live. Sometime later, I ran into her out at the mailboxes and she greeted me with: "Well, it's been three months now. I'm officially no longer here."

She not only continued to live, she flourished. As much as possible, she ignored her frailties and continued caring for her gardens and her dogs. And then one day, she crashed. She went from reasonably active to waking up one morning knowing she was at the end. She declined swiftly over that day and told her daughter, "If I do my job right, I won't be here tomorrow." Sandy called to let us know, and we visited that evening to sit with Dora for a bit and say good-bye. She was just barely awake, enough to know that we and our dog, Timiah—she loved Timiah—were there. She had been my first non-family massage client when I was still in training, and I did some gentle massage on her back that night. When we left, I told Sandy I'd come over in the very early morning to take over for her, so she could get some rest.

Well before dawn, I got up, walked down their long driveway, and let myself in their front door. All was dark and quiet. Even the dogs, normally vocal with visitors, were silent as I walked past them to Dora's room at the back of the house. Her light was off, too, and there was no sign of Sandy. I turned on a light in the room next to Dora's so that I could see her. Of course, she had died. Not long after we'd left the night before, I later learned. Sandy had notified their hospice nurse and gone to bed. I stood at the foot of Dora's bed for a few minutes, wishing her well and saying another good-bye, and then went home.

Our writings have focused mostly on the concept of being with dying, of getting comfortable with the idea that we and those around us will die, and perhaps becoming more accepting and even graceful. Absent from most of our discussions, though, has been the more concrete matter of being with death, that is, with someone who has just died. With a body. The corpse.

It is what we all will be at some point, but the dead body is so imbued with frightful associations that for many people it probably is hard to imagine being in a room or a house with one. And yet, when someone close has died, it can be hard to leave the room or to have the body removed. Sandy, for instance, was comfortable going to bed for some much-needed sleep, with her mother's body two rooms away. That physical part of the person is still there, something to hold on to for a brief moment before the rituals we have created for death's immediate aftermath take over. Wakes, cremation, embalming, sitting shiva, burial, scattering—all rituals, all ways we have devised to feel that we've done well by our loved one's soul and body. And before they come into play, there are those minutes, perhaps longer, of just being with the body and with death.

I've told you the story of my Dad's death, of not making the decision to be with him immediately upon learning of his heart attack and hospitalization and so missing the moment of his death. When I did arrive and went into his hospital room, the others in my family had just left, so it was me alone with his body, which was still hooked up to machines to keep his organs operating in case there was a transplant possibility.

I stood next to his bed, watching his chest rise and fall and trying to reconcile that with the fact that he was dead. I now wish I had spent more time with him then, but I know it was important for me to see him and spend even those few moments with his body. That's odd in a way, because he has been buried in a cemetery in Massachusetts for nearly thirty years now, and though it is barely two hours away, I've been to his grave only a handful of times. My father's final resting is very important to me, but it is not that small plot of earth a half hour north of Boston. It is in my mind, in my heart, and I visit with him quite often.

Back to his body. It meant something for me to see him, if briefly, after he'd died. He might not have been able to hear me, but I still got a chance to say good-bye, and to touch him. I said good-bye in my own way, and under the circumstances it had to suffice. I wonder if the urge to see and touch a loved one who has died is universal. Whether it is or not, it is generally overtaken, for better or worse, by ritual. What happens to a body after death differs from culture to culture, but it is often all about ritual, which is something humans have been using as a source of comfort for millennia, isn't it?

It was interesting to me to read a collection of essays by Thomas Lynch, an American funeral director and writer, called *Bodies in Motion and at Rest: On Metaphor and Mortality*.[1] In one essay, he writes about this culture's evolving perspective on the minutes and days after a death. If you'll pardon the long quotation:

> Whether we burn or bury our dead or blast them into space is less important than what we do before we dispose of them. More and more, we care for our own dying. More and more we are making up new liturgies to say good-bye. More and more we seem willing to engage fully in

the process of leave-taking. We rise early to watch the TV obsequies of princesses and modern saints. We read the obits every day. We eulogize, elegize and memorialize with vigor. The trade is brisk in wakes and funerals. We sell copper and combustibles, bronze and biodegradables, eco-friendly and economy models. We do urns that look like golf bags and go to cemeteries with names like golf courses. You can buy a casket off the Internet, or buy plans for a self-built coffin table or one that doubles as a bookshelf or armoire until you "need" it. There is a kind of push for "do-it-yourself" funerals, as if grief were anything but. Cremated remains can be cast into bookends, or paper weights or duck decoys. They can be recycled as memorial cat litter, sprinkled on our rose bushes, mixed with oil paints to add texture to fresh masterpieces. We have, as Batesville Casket Company calls its latest marketing approach, "Options." . . . The expanding choices in mortuary wares make it seem as if we really have choices about mortality.[2]

The choices we have are all related to those rituals. Not dying is not among the options, and maybe nothing makes that clearer than a few minutes or hours being with, sitting with, and putting one's hands on death.

Our plans to hold our first Café mortel at your house next month seem to be coming along nicely. I know we don't plan to direct the conversation too much, but I'll be interested to see if people want to talk about their experiences or perspectives regarding the human body, post-life.

S.

Lebanon, NH
3 May 2012

Dear Steve,

It's almost midnight, but I just had to write to you before our upcoming meeting on Sunday, our attempt at one of Crettaz's Cafés mortels. For reasons I'll explain shortly, I feel like I haven't had a free moment since I first opened your e-mail three weeks ago.

I am fascinated by the topic you raised there of our relationship to actual dead bodies and feel like I have a lot to share. I just couldn't get to sharing it sooner, because I guess you could say I was so busy having related experiences. I'm glad we're friends and can talk on these topics and yet somehow I feel like it's also important to recognize and acknowledge the differences between us and how they affect our approach to these issues. For instance, your last letter was filled with thoughts of spring and death, and yet you didn't mention one word about Easter, the holiday most connected, at least in the Christian world, to the topics of spring and death—and life. I know you to be a deeply spiritual being, but not necessarily a religious one, if you'll permit me the distinction, and in any case not a frequent churchgoer. So I hope it's okay to note that Easter was celebrated this year in the Western churches right before you wrote (April 8) and in my church, the Eastern Orthodox tradition, a week later (April 15).

Please don't misunderstand me; my pointing that out is meant only as a reminder of our different orientations. We Eastern Orthodox Christians hold literally more than a dozen services during Holy Week. Hopefully, thinking about the true meaning and relationship of life and death is the complete focus of our lives for at least that week. We rediscover that God did not intend death for his creation and that Jesus's encounter with death destroyed death. As our Paschal hymn says: "Christ tramples down death by death, bestowing life on those in the tombs." There's a marvelous book explaining this mystery by Father Alexander Schmemann called *O Death, Where Is Thy Sting?* (a quote from the epistles of Paul).[3] Interestingly, the book is mainly based on the English translation of broadcasts Father Schmemann made into the Soviet Union during the Cold War to explain true Christian tenants to his fellow Russians. I could tell you more about it if you're interested. During our Holy Week this year, the father of a dear friend died as well. I felt so sad when I realized I didn't have the energy to drive several hundred miles to his funeral in between the Easter services; I knew and loved him, as well as his daughter, and would have been there under any other circumstances.

To explain my long silence further, after barely managing to get my taxes done while attending all those church services—a very complicated splitting of attention for me most years—I left the country to accompany Dartmouth alumni on a trip to the Netherlands and Belgium. That was great. I've never seen so many beautiful tulips or old cities in one go. What was even more wonderful is that I was able to visit at the end of the trip with my sister Maria (whose husband Steve you've heard so much about). And get this; while she and I were in Amsterdam, we just happened to "bump into" not one but three exhibitions related to the topic of death. When I learned of them, I was very eager to go because of the sharing you and I have been doing about mortality. I worried, though, that spending time explicitly exploring death would be too much for my sister. However, Maria encouraged my interest and insisted on accompanying me. My deep hope is that some of it might have helped her in the mourning process. I'm wanting to tell you about it all at once, but let me finish accounting for my silence by sharing that I've only returned from Europe yesterday, and the next two days I will be at an annual department seminar. All this is by way of saying that tonight is my only chance to respond to what you've written before our meeting on Sunday when perhaps our focus will change once again.

Okay, so to dead bodies. I think I've already mentioned to you that because of how our mother grew up in a small Greek village, she had a high level of familiarity and comfort with the dying and the dead. No doubt I have not had the number of opportunities to be with dead bodies that my mother's had, but still, I feel thankful that because of her, I did have some contact, even as a young kid, contact that I guess many of my American schoolmates did not have. I believe I specifically told you about our mother taking me and my sisters when we were still little squirts to the wake of a neighbor we knew and liked. I recall also telling you about my paternal grandfather dying of a heart attack when he was only sixty-five and I was twelve. There was an open coffin at the funeral. I realized that that was the body of my beloved grandfather. Still, I'd be lying if I claimed not to have had any trepidation as we were told to approach it and kiss him at the end of the service. Thinking back to it now, I believe that at least some of my fear was generated by the incredibly high level of emotional distress in the church—my grandmother screaming that he should open his eyes and not leave her; my father so agitated that he couldn't sit—rather than by the corpse itself. Still, I registered that my grandfather didn't look or feel the same and that somehow I'd never see him again. By the way, as "Greek" as we were, we grandchildren were not allowed to go to the cemetery; I remember that being communicated to us with the hidden message that burials were too scary for kids. Which, as you can tell, was another difference to how our mother was brought up. . . . Come to think of it, I'm not sure why our seeing the actual burial was judged by the adults to be scarier than seeing a dead body in a casket or having to kiss it. But I assume it's the act of putting the casket in the ground and seeing dirt thrown on it. That does seem more "final" than seeing the dead body, I guess.

I doubt you're eager for a recital of all the dead bodies I've seen or not seen, so I promise not to give one. I do have the urge to mention that on some occasions of the deaths of people I have deeply loved, I did not manage to see the corpse or coffin or urn at any point in the postmortem, and I believe that that made those losses and processing them even harder. It won't surprise you to learn that one of those cases was when the Zantops were killed. I think I was in such a state of shock that it never occurred to me to ask: where are their bodies now? This question entered my consciousness only when, several days after their actual murder, another friend said that she had gone to the morgue with members of the family. I was filled with a new sadness that I had not taken leave of their physical remains. While I don't think I could have articulated it at that point in my life, I suspect I had already arrived at a stage where I valued being with the dead. Or maybe it was precisely because of that missed experience that I then started consciously valuing a physical leave-taking.

136 LET'S TALK ABOUT DEATH

And that leads me to one of the exhibitions I saw with Maria in Amsterdam. It was called "Death Matters" and was shown in the Tropenmuseum, or Museum of the Tropics. As you know, the Netherlands had quite an empire at one point, and this museum concerns itself in many, though not all, regards with places very different from Holland. That was reflected in this exhibition, as it tried to show customs related to death and mourning from a large number of geographically and historically diverse cultures. I imagine it resembled the show Crettaz and his associates put together in Geneva. In Amsterdam there was, for instance, a display of objects, "vehicles" actually, used by various cultures to send their dead on their journey to the afterlife. There was assorted clothing—some old, some contemporary, some Western, some not—for mourners themselves. I love fabrics and found myself fascinated by the variety of colors deemed appropriate for those grieving. The part that really stopped me in my tracks, though, was a display of photographs by Walter Schels, a German photographer who, with journalist Beate Lakotta, had received permission to accompany individuals dying in hospice. In each case the dying had agreed to be photographed and interviewed while alive and to be photographed again in the time shortly after their deaths. The display consisted, then, of a series of two paired, large-format, black-and-white photos of the same individual; captions listed their names and the dates on which the photos were taken. Not surprisingly, the images were of very high quality, and that added to my desire to keep looking at them. To me, these photos created a sacred experience. Standing in front of them, I felt almost overwhelmed by the beauty captured there, the beauty of the individual alive and also dead. As much as the two subjects of the two photos in any pair resembled each other, there was also a profound difference. In some cases there was a physical change that you could describe. I remember being struck by the photos of a very young child; in the portrait of the deceased child, you could see some kind of dried matter at the end of the child's eyelashes. But mostly it was hard to pinpoint what was different besides the closed eyes. And yet it was there. "It" was death. My own inability to describe, label, or process it, humbled me.

Alas, there was no English version of the catalog for the whole exhibition; I've been kicking myself for not having bought the Dutch version. However, there is a book of Schels and Lakotta's larger photo-text project titled, *Noch mal leben: Eine Ausstellung über das Sterben* which means literally "To Live Again: An Exhibition about Dying." The show itself has been translated into English as "Life before Death," and, in addition to Amsterdam, has been hosted in a large number of German cities, as well as venues in Austria, Switzerland, Sweden, Israel, Japan, and Canada (Montreal). I find it fascinating that it hasn't come to the United States. I plan to order the book that resulted from the project and exhibition soon. In the meantime, you could learn more about "Noch mal leben" and see some of the photos on the Internet.[4] I'd love to discuss it with you. Or maybe we can do that once I receive the book. It includes these individuals' thoughts as well as their portraits, and it would be wonderful to learn what people wanted to share at a point when they knew their deaths were imminent—the kind of thoughts that you're privy to more often than most people because of your work with Hand to Heart.

The other two exhibitions were at a Dutch cemetery a little farther from the center of town. In a small building near the entrance, there were various types of contemporary art works dealing with the artists' imaginings of encounters with the dead. I don't remember as many details as from the Tropics Museum, but I do recall one very large installation that depicted the artist's sense of the traumatic deaths of 9/11. Another was a long video interview with a child who seemed to have encounters with people who had passed on. And a third—I think this was part of the standing exhibition—had various historical objects related to morticians and private and public mourning rituals, like objects made out of the deceased's hair.

What was most engaging for my sister and me were the artworks installed outside, in various locations within the cemetery grounds. It was a bit like a treasure hunt to find them from the map given to us, and along the way it was quite interesting to look at the tombstones—much more varied in materials, shapes, and messages than those in any cemetery I'd seen in the States. As for the "official" artwork, I remember one subterranean installation where if you sat still in the middle of this underground space, you could see a projection onto its ceiling of the area directly above it, that is, above ground, in a rather faint—dare I say ghostly?—way; there was a rather-complicated mathematical explanation of how that image got produced, though as a spectator, one didn't really need to understand the science of it to feel the impact of being below the earth and seeing what was above you. Another installation consisted of the peeling bark of a hollow, inside-out tree trunk; not quite sure how the artist did that, given the size of the trunk. A third was a small trailer you could enter that had only one chair in it. There was tango music playing, and projected onto the walls was video footage of individuals who were dancing solo, but as if there was someone in their arms. Maria was very affected by this and started to cry, so of course I started to cry, too. Which was fine. I started worrying again, though, that it wasn't fair of me to let her come. Well, that sounds like I think I know best. I don't mean that, I realize now. Based on my own experiences, I think the mourner knows best. Maria told me that she found the artwork of the dancers to correspond closest to her experience. She feels like she has to dance solo now, and while she keeps moving, sometimes it feels very lonely.

It's almost 3 a.m. and I'd better get some sleep so I can be coherent at the seminar. I'll see you Sunday afternoon at my house. Like you, I'm really curious about who will come and what topics they'll want to discuss.

Yours,

i.

Cornish, NH
May 9, 2012

Dear Irene,

Your descriptions of the exhibitions you saw on your trip made them sound fascinating. And they remind me of another exhibition, one that

I and a great many other people saw a few years ago as it made its way through quite a few cities in North America. It was called "Body Worlds," the creation of Gunther von Hagens, a German man who had developed a technique called "plastination," in which cadavers are infused with a material that preserves them indefinitely and allows them to be placed into all manner of poses. I wrote about it in the *Valley News*.[5] For "Body Worlds," von Hagens had collected the corpses of dozens and dozens of people (and some animals, including a horse, a camel, and a gorilla), usually stripping off the skin and often peeling back layers of muscle to reveal the inner life, if you will, of human beings' bodies. Some were placed into active poses: figure skaters, soccer players, divers, and the like. Some were in more static poses, such as the one reminiscent of Rodin's *The Thinker*, except his back had been laid open to reveal the strata of muscle and bone. To a massage therapist like myself, it was incredible, though one thought I had at the time is that the world is clearly divided into two groups: people who are comfortable in a roomful of marginally lifelike cadavers, and people who are not.

Gunther von Hagens met a lot of resistance when developing the exhibition, first at home in Germany and later in many of the places the show was set up. People were sometimes offended by the supposed desecration of human bodies. It was an understandable reaction, I guess; there was once life behind those eyes, electricity in those nerves. It could be discomfiting to see them preserved to be stared at. Some church leaders tried to have the exhibition shut down in their cities, or prevented from opening.

Visiting an exhibition of artfully displayed bodies is different from being with the body of a loved one who has just died. But looking back, I think the "Body Worlds" dispute was a good example of our cultural uncertainty about bodies. What do we do with them? Bury them immediately? Incinerate them? Fill them with a cocktail of chemicals to "preserve" them? Donate them to science? Embalming has been around forever, but why? The deceased gets nothing from that tradition. What do survivors get? As I've mentioned to you, I attended a lot of wakes in my Catholic childhood, and I remember well that the embalmed body never really looked like the deceased, except in a wax-museum-y way. The lines were always wrong. The distinction between the hands, for instance, one resting on the other, was blurred, as if they'd been carved from a big bar of soap by someone who wasn't confident with details. Still, there was never any question in my extended family that the deceased, any deceased, would be embalmed. I didn't even know about cremation through most of my youth.

When my grandmother died several years ago—yes, the sometimes cranky one you've heard a bit about—she had little money left to cover funeral expenses and had agreed that cremation was acceptable to her. I remember that at the calling hours, many members of her family, especially older ones, were unhappy that they were paying their respects to an urn of ashes and not a casket with a body in it.

I assume that the rituals we have developed for handling the bodies of people who have died help lend a feeling of routine to death, which can seem anything but routine when it happens close to us. I know that despite my family background, I have no interest in being embalmed after I die. Cremation has always seemed reasonable to me, although I know some people have problems with that, as well. A Tibetan-style sky burial, with the body left high on a mountainside to be devoured by birds and have its spirit, or essence, sent into the ether, has an ultra-natural appeal, but probably isn't a good option in New England. I would want what happens to my body to be as natural as my death itself. Maybe that's why fire seems appropriate and embalming doesn't.

Before the group discussing it at our Café mortel and me writing this today, I don't think I'd spent much time wondering what should happen to a body after death—from the moments after to the days after to the eternity after—so my thoughts as I've put them down here are feeling a little scattered.

In 1908 Rainer Maria Rilke—a poet we've talked about before—wrote his "Requiem for a Friend" after a close friend had died during childbirth. I found it online when I was looking for another of his writings. He wrote it a year after her death, as though she were appearing before him, a vision or a ghost or a too-vivid memory. He is addressing her, wondering not just why she died but how he and others should have mourned her:

> And so you died as women used to die, at home, in your own warm bedroom, the old-fashioned death of women in labor, who try to close themselves again but can't, because that ancient darkness which they have also given birth to returns for them, thrusts its way in, and enters. Once ritual lament would have been chanted; women would have been paid to beat their breasts and howl for you all night, when all is silent. Where can we find such customs now? So many have long since disappeared or been disowned. That's what you had to come for: to retrieve the lament that we omitted.[6]

As for our Café mortel gathering at your home last week, I thought it was a great beginning. Nearly a dozen of us conversing comfortably about death and mortality. Everyone there was a friend of either yours or mine, so they came in with whatever information we had given them about what to expect. Still, since we didn't know what to expect, they didn't either. I didn't have the feeling that any of them had specific ideas of what they hoped to gain from the gathering. In the end, it was so comfortable that the time we'd allotted flew by, ending, I suspect, while most of us still had things we wanted to say. I was especially intrigued by the way some in the group likened death to birth, in that both are major life events for which it can be good to have a plan. In both cases, how the event actually plays out might be quite different from the plan, and in neither case is that necessarily important. The value, the comfort, is in the planning itself. It was also interesting to see that many of those present said they weren't afraid of dying as much as of being in pain as they approach death. Fits right in with what you and I have been exploring and discovering in our letters, doesn't it?

We'll have another chance to explore and discover at the next gathering in June, it looks like. Meanwhile, I will be interested to see where you take our conversation next.

Steve

Lebanon, NH
22 May 2012

Hi, Steve,

Big day over here. Philippe just left for his long summer stay in his hometown in Switzerland. I'll be able to join him in July, but I'm always amazed at how much I miss him despite having shared this rhythm of separations and reunions for so many years, despite all the things I need to get done and can get done once he's gone and the hours of the day we normally share are available for work-related activities. After dropping him at the bus this morning, I raced to school for a meeting, and after the meeting there was a spectacular reading by writer Louise Erdrich. You probably know that she's a Dartmouth alum and used to live around here. We're lucky that she cares to come back every now and then. Of course it helps that her daughter decided to study here. Have you ever read any of Erdrich's books? I'm a huge fan of what I've had time to read, my favorite being a carnivalesque tale called *The Last Report on the Miracles at Little No Horse*, about the interactions of the Catholic Church and the Ojibwe tribe on a remote reservation.[7] I read it years ago before I found myself reflecting explicitly on life and death, life with death, but come to think of it, that novel has a lot to say on our subject, too. Today Erdrich regaled us—the largest auditorium at Dartmouth was packed from bottom to top—with some excerpts from a forthcoming novel called *The Round House*, to be released this fall.[8] Erdrich has a great reading voice, and I could have listened to her all night. The parts she read to us definitely had to do with passions and violence and the threat of death. In fact, there was an interesting variation on a theme you've raised in one of our earlier exchanges: one character needs a transplant and tries to get it from an estranged sibling—his twin, actually—whom he and their mother have rejected all her life. I can't wait to see how that fits into the larger novel.

Of all the intriguing topics you brought up in your last e-mail, maybe I'll start with the basic issue of comfort in simply being with a corpse. When exactly, do you suppose, Americans became so uncomfortable with real dead bodies? We're obsessed with showing them in movies and on television, of course. Yet, I suspect that other than police, emergency workers, medical personnel, and those in the funeral industries, few Americans can say they've spent more than brief moments in the presence of a corpse. If Jessica Mitford and her reports on the American funeral industry—*The American Way of Death* is from 1963 and an update was published as the *American Way of Death Revisited* in 1998—are as well-researched as they seem to be, it sounds to me like this banishing of the dead body is actually a pretty recent development from the second half of the twentieth century.[9] From my own observations and Mitford's, though, it's an uneven ban in the Western world, depending on your exact location, religion, and subculture.

I think the book that makes me worry the most about abandoning bodies as soon as the breath is out of them, so to speak, is Simone de Beauvoir's celebrated reflection about her mother's passing: *Une Mort très douce* (1964; the American edition, *A Very Easy Death*, appeared in 1966).[10] I think two of the elements that readers find so compelling about de Beauvoir's account concern parent-child relations and medical treatment. Simone was a black sheep in her family, and yet on many levels she's a very attentive, caring presence in her mother's dying. As for medical interventions, especially for the elderly and the very ill: Françoise, the mother, is diagnosed with cancer—though nobody ever explains that to her—and her doctors seem more fascinated with all the things they can try to do to intervene than with the patient's comfort. Her pain is terrific and mostly goes untreated. In other words, it's not an easy death at all. However, the point I want to share with you revolves around the moments after Françoise has finally died. Even though the mother herself supposedly rejects the idea that a cadaver means anything, is anything, or has anything to do with the person who was once alive, Simone is not so sure that she feels good about having abandoned her mother's body. After all, the daughter writes, "it was her skin, her bones, and for a little while longer her face. My father, I stayed close to him until the moment where he did become for me an object; I tamed the passage from presence to non-existence. With Mom, I left almost as soon as I had kissed her, and that's why it seemed to me that it was still her person who was lying alone in the cold of the morgue."[11]

I think I can try to explain my own view about being with dead bodies if I make one more detour to a very different kind of book I read recently. It's a philosophical study of attitudes toward death by a British scholar named Benjamin Noys titled *The Culture of Death* (2005).[12] His main analysis concerns our contemporary global society, with regard specifically to our exposure to mass annihilation and the concept of bare life (put forward by the Italian philosopher Giorgio Agamben). As interesting as I found Noys's larger argument, what I want to share with you is a very specific part of the book where he reflects on the medical-technological developments that led to new views of comas as well as new possibilities for organ transplants. You and I have been living most of our conscious lives in the aftermath of these developments, so it might come as a surprise to you, as it did to me, that the idea of "brain death" is actually quite recent (a Harvard committee published a report on this in 1968).[13] What I really appreciate about Noys's analysis is that he shows that previous understandings of when someone is dead (no breathing, no heart beat) have been replaced by a concept that is much more slippery. I'm not interested in getting into ethical or legal debates about transplants if I don't have to. (I've already declared my desire for any part of my body to be harvested that might help another human being.) For me, learning these things resulted quite concretely in internalizing that the moment of death is much more uncertain than I'd thought previously. It also resulted

WHAT COMES AFTER I DIE?   145

in my determination for the future that if at all possible, I'd like to simply "be" with the dead body of a loved one as long as I am able. I don't think it's possible to decide in advance how long a time that will be, but as de Beauvoir's conscience was telling her in the aftermath of her hasty departure from her mother's corpse, "it" was still her mother for a while longer, and on some level, she had abandoned her. To my mind, even if we thought of the physical matter of the body as the mere means by which someone was able to do his or her "work" and "loving" in the world, wouldn't we want to honor that pile of matter? Don't I want to honor that material body? By the way, I see Walter Schels's photographs that I told you about a few weeks ago as some kind of illustration of this reflection of de Beauvoir: for a little while, anyway, it's still the same person, already starting to transform, perhaps, but still identifiably a person. I think. . . .

There is an enormous amount of very beautiful hymnography in the Eastern Orthodox Christian tradition about Joseph of Arimathea and Nicodemus, who took care of Jesus's body after his death by crucifixion, daring to ask Pilate for the body of this disgraced individual, anointing it with spices, wrapping it in a clean shroud, and placing it in a new tomb. There are also many hymns of praise for the women who wanted to anoint Jesus's entombed body with myrrh (hence, they're usually referred to as the Myrrh-bearers). Through their desire to anoint Jesus at the first oppor-tunity after the Sabbath, they are blessed to learn of the Resurrection. Mary, one of these Myrrh-bearers, is reported in the Gospel of John to be the first person to actually see the risen Christ (John 20:14–18).

You might remember that some of us at the Café mortel talked about a book we'd read on burial in the ancient Christian tradition by J. Mark Barna and Elizabeth Barna.[14] What they write there about taking care of the deceased person's body follows the outline of how Jesus's body was treated. Even for today's world, this makes so much sense to me. I've heard the arguments for cremation as more ecologically friendly than burial. However, after reading about the cremation process—bones don't burn, you have to crush them with huge amounts of force to turn them into dust—and on one's legal rights to a simple burial in the earth—no embalming, no coffin or just a very simple wooden one if required—I've changed my view. I'm delighted about the green burial movement, and unless a complicated set of unforeseen circumstances would require it, I'd like to be buried simply and at the nearest available place so that not too much fuel is used to get my body there.[15]

Whoah! I feel calm writing this to you, but I also realize that I feel a bit weighed down right now. Maybe I'm feeling the earth above me already?

Write back soon,

Yours,

Irene

Cornish, NH

May 26, 2012

Dear Irene,

Interesting that you mention Jessica Mitford and her book about the funeral industry. Thomas Lynch, the funeral director and author I quoted earlier, writes about her at length in the book I referenced. He seems to like her and understand where her critique is coming from, but ultimately he takes her to task for not understanding the human need for ritual and for other services offered by morticians. He claims that while she was very critical of the high price of funerals, those costs had risen at a slower rate than most other things in our society over previous decades. Lynch also got to know Mitford's adult children after she died and pointed out that despite her interest in small, simple, and inexpensive funerals, they and other family members staged a couple of large and extravagant memorial services for her. They told him that in their view, the services weren't for their mother, but for those who were still alive. So they didn't worry about what she would have wanted, had she had a voice.[16]

I saw Lynch as pretty defensive in that particular essay, but the dispute does make clear to me that nothing will ever be all that simple when it comes to what people decide to do with the bodies of their loved ones. Which is a shame, because simple seemed to be the important point behind what you wrote about preferring to spend time with the body just after death—before the death industry steps in, in whatever way it will. Many spiritual traditions believe that the soul or life essence is in or near the body for some time after death, and certainly the important emotional connection with the just-deceased doesn't end with the last heartbeat or the last measurable brain wave, so you could be sitting with more than a body, anyway.

In her 2003 book *Stiff: The Curious Lives of Human Cadavers*, Mary Roach explores the many ways humans have treated, mistreated, studied, and disposed of bodies.[17] From efforts in France to see if a just-guillotined head could still communicate, to a corpse "farm" in the United States used to study decomposition and insect invasions for use in crime solving, the book covers a lot of fascinating and absurd ground. One study I particularly liked was by a scientist who wanted to prove not only that the soul did exist, but also that it had measurable substance. He placed people near death on a bed that was sitting on a large scale. His goal was to show that people lose just a bit of weight immediately after death, which he would have attributed to the departure of the soul. His results were inconclusive, I gather.

It reminds me of the trouble that Andreas Vesalius—the sixteenth-century anatomist whose work revolutionized the study of human biology and also influenced the man who 540 or so years later developed the "Body Worlds" exhibit I mentioned earlier—got into with the Vatican. The church had at various times over the centuries either banned or approved of dissections of human bodies, but at the time Vesalius was cutting into corpses to catalog their contents, he was doing so with, if not the blessing of the church, at least the protection of some powerful political figures. It was expected that in his work, he would find the "resurrection bone," an actual structure that held the spark that would allow for eventual resurrection, and that was assumed to exist in the human body. He did not, which didn't sit well with the authorities.[18]

The resurrection bone is a great concept, though, isn't it? A physical entity that connects us to the eternity that awaits us. Without it we are left to our beliefs and best guesses as to what will happen to the nonphysical aspects of our selves after death.

You were right to make note of the differences between us when it comes to religion and spirituality. I was a Catholic as a child and have been affiliated with a couple of Protestant churches as an adult, but these days I have no clear idea of what comes after life. Churches that define God and good in very narrow ways are not credible to me, even if I do envy their certainty. What I understand to be very powerful belief is, to those churches and people, more than believing. It is knowing. It is certainty about something that I know (or believe?) to be unknowable. There must be a lot of comfort in having no doubt about your image of God, your sense of how to live your life, and your notion of what is in store for you after you die.

I have only questions and doubts. I can't separate the doctrine of the church I grew up in from the historical and current facts: that through the centuries that church has been as much a political entity as a religious one, and that a great many horrible things have been done in its name. So I can't assume that its doctrinal teachings, including on dying, death, and the afterlife, are any more reliable than the rest of its record.

Is there a heaven? Or a hell? Is my Dad somewhere out there, aware of or watching over my life? (Gulp.) I have a friend who has gone through the process, using hypnosis, of connecting not just with what she believes are her previous lives, but with a space between those lives, an actual place where souls go between "assignments" in this world, a place governed by enlightened beings trying to guide each soul to its own state of enlightenment. It seems far-fetched to me, but if you put an outline of that belief next to outlines of more mainstream belief systems, and presented them to someone with no previous exposure to any of them, would my friend's be the only one that seemed far-fetched?

These questions about what happens to our souls or our life essences, of whether there still might be a resurrection bone to be found, if only a metaphorical one, can make questions about what do with a corpse seem pretty simple. But religion and spirituality are so much a part of human history and consciousness that there's no doubt they have as much influence over our feelings about death and mortality as anything else in our lives.

S.

Lebanon, NH
Monday, 4 June 2012

Hi there,

Want to get my thoughts down before the onslaught of yet another week at school. Dartmouth goes so over the top with activities at the end of the academic year; I've got one meeting after another all week long.

I thought our second Café mortel yesterday afternoon was amazing. At first I felt a little sad that we were such a small group, as if we'd failed somehow to sustain interest. Actually, it seems more like people are just so busy these days. I know a lot of my friends who didn't return had loved the first session and simply couldn't fit this in right now. (In the spirit of "full disclosure," one of them found the previous discussion too depressing and didn't want to do that to herself again.) Certainly those of us who were there yesterday shared on profound and difficult subjects. I thought it was particularly fascinating (if not exactly surprising) that many of the issues you and I have been exchanging thoughts on were brought up by others in the group, without our prompting, like what experiences we'd had with death as children, saying farewell to the dead, the funeral industry. I guess you and I are not so unique in our preoccupations and, further, that we Americans do not have enough venues to talk about mortality. So given one, we run with it.

I found the many stories folks shared about *first* contacts with death to be particularly moving because it was so obvious how those initial experiences had shaped subsequent lives and developing attitudes toward mortality. A pattern seemed to be that if parents were in denial about the reality of death, then it was hard for kids to be otherwise, especially if all questions posed or explanations asked for were immediately shut down. I haven't had a chance to check if there's an English translation or simply a similar book, but last summer in our local library in Switzerland I found a slim volume called *La Mort expliquée à ma fille*, which would translate as "Death Explained to My Daughter."[19] I was struck by the book's straightforward tone and the author's explicit effort not to dramatize or make any part of the subject taboo. When I wrote to you a while back of my exploration of the work of Bernard Crettaz, I forgot to tell you that an offshoot of that big exhibition they did on death in Geneva was a book for children. It's a really clever story about the young-adult son of a mortician who finds himself taking over for his father when the father dies unexpectedly. I got it out of the Lausanne university library and read it. It seemed to me very accessible to young people because of its plotline and characters, almost all of whom display an incredibly matter-of-fact attitude toward death. Maybe it's weird because I'm not the target audience, but come to think of it again, I loved that book and ponder its message often. (It has the same title as the exposition, *La Mort à vivre*.)[20]

Of course it caught my attention during our chat yesterday that others also wanted to talk about being with the corpse and truly taking leave of the person. And yet, it was clear, wasn't it, that many of them really can't see themselves wanting much physical contact with dead bodies and can't warm to the idea of having their loved ones give them postmortem care, like washing and dressing the body? I find myself going in the opposite direction and am chomping at the bit, so to speak, to learn more about how individuals and small groups are taking it on themselves to assume responsibility for the bodies of the dead, rather than turning them over to funeral professionals. For instance, I'd like to read more about the new energy in New York, at least as reported in the *New York Times*, for lay

Jewish teams to care for the deceased, by bathing, dressing, praying for, and watching over them.[21] Also I'm eager to find answers to some of the questions we had about what the local laws are with regard to embalming and burial practices. I love the vision you shared yesterday of little teams all over the Upper Valley who could be on call to offer volunteer help to prepare the body for transport and burial when someone dies.

As for our exchanges here, I definitely got the impression from your last missive that you want us—meaning at least you and me now—to discuss "after death." Am I right about that? I get your complaints about organized religion, especially—with any residual due respect—about the Catholic Church. Sexual abuse on the part of ordained clergy seems even more widespread than the most cynical of us would have believed. It depresses me greatly. And of course wars in the name of religion, especially in the name of Christ, have never made any sense to me at all. These mistakes of human origin, however, don't lead me to abandon my own sense of the Divine, or of the possible value of religious tradition. You might find it interesting to reread your first message to me in this sequence; you refer to "ritual" over and over; so maybe somewhere deep inside, you, too, wonder if all those religions that profess that death is not an absolute end might be onto something.

I feel like I should confess to you that as much as I thought I had a relatively healthy and informed attitude toward mortality, it wasn't until the Zantops were murdered that I directly asked myself, So what does my church believe about what happens after death? I found out about the crime on a Saturday night, cried all through the night, and at the earliest possible moment in the morning, I called my priest. It was a bit of a blur then and hence is still now, but he told me I could come to church right away, and he spoke to me as soon as I arrived. I remember that in addition to crying hysterically, I kept asking him what I should do. He told me which Psalm is traditionally recited (Psalm 119) and sent someone to retrieve a copy of the Bible from our little church library downstairs. At some point that same Sunday, or another time—again, it's all rather a blur—the priest and I spoke again, and strange as it is to admit at my age (or even my age then), that's when I realized, when I truly took in what I'd been passively hearing all my life: that we do not believe in the immediate ascension of the person to God (unless you're a saint). Rather, we believe that the human person sleeps until the Second Coming. I guess I've been on a long, slow journey since then, trying to put together the familiar rituals of our religion around death—praying that God forgive the deceased every sin and remember them when He comes into His Kingdom; praying at certain anniversaries from the time of death (forty days, one year, three years, etc.); praying at certain points in the regular liturgy and at certain special services in the Church year for the memory of the dead, like in preparation for Easter, and so on—with reading more about our theological beliefs. I think I could summarize what I've learned so far by repeating that God never intended death for humankind; that it was humankind who refused intimate contact with the Divine, thus bringing death into the world; that it was Jesus Christ's role to destroy death and put humankind back into relationship with the Divine; and that we believe we will truly be reunited at the end of the world. Yet it's simply not our role to know exactly when or how that will happen.

So, sorry to disappoint, but I guess the certainty you assume is out there for believers is only operative for us Orthodox in some domains, definitely not in others. We know human death is not the end, but exactly what's next, well, that's less clear. We just know it's going to be glorious because we will be united to the Source of Love. There is a book I can recommend if you want more of a sense of religious faith on the part of Orthodox Christians that death is not the end. It's called *Lynette's Hope*, and it was actually put together by a cousin of mine, Luke Veronis, who is a priest and served for many years as a missionary in Albania.[22] One of his fellow missionaries there, a young woman named Lynette Hoppe, received a diagnosis of invasive breast cancer. She aggressively pursued all possible treatments, but they could not hold her cancer in abeyance. Luke uses writings by Lynette and others who loved her, as well as his own recollections, to recount her final journey. What's very striking in the book is the cultural context: it appears that Albanians are particularly allergic to talking about death. Everyone who had contact with Lynette was therefore astounded by how openly she came to speak of her impending death. And they were all blown away by her unshakable belief in her reunion with the Divine. She not only died peacefully, but, according to those present, thirty minutes later developed a glorious smile on her face. In addition to my cousin's book, there are many related Internet postings on Lynette.[23] These testimonies to Lynette's faith and how she used it to positively affect others are inspiring to me as I query myself about the quality of my faith.

I'm sure you, like I, have heard about and perhaps even read some of the books by individuals who have been declared clinically dead and then come back to life. Many people, especially, it seems, those who know they are likely to die soon, take great comfort from these reports of luminous tunnels, reunions with loved ones, and so on. For example, the French psychiatrist David Servan-Schreiber who died last summer and whose book I read and told you about has a long passage on near-death experiences; he describes being very comforted by what he thinks they bode for his own after-death.[24] I don't think I told you about a full-length narrative I also read called *90 Minutes in Heaven* by an American pastor named Don Piper (2004; apropos of my comments above, with an edition for "young readers" that came out in 2009).[25] Piper was in an absolutely horrific car accident and was pronounced dead at the scene. Another minister who was held up in the traffic that backed up near the accident asked the rescuers what was going on, and when he was told one man was dead, he felt a call to pray. He went to what was supposed to be a corpse and began praying for Piper. Eventually he felt a pulse and insisted that the first responders get Piper out of the car and to the hospital. Piper himself, he tells us, was in heaven all that time. Frankly, the paradise he describes having been in is about as stereotypical an image of heaven as our society has put together: all the people he'd known and loved who had died were there to greet him, the light was brilliant and beautiful, there was a gate to be ushered through with a luminosity on the other side like none he'd ever seen on Earth, ditto for the music. I think you get the idea. I've already told you, my belief system doesn't subscribe to most of us going straight to God. However, I guess it's also in my belief system to accept that others might have experiences that I simply can't fathom, and I'm putting Piper's in that category. Though it might surprise you about a university professor, I also try not to make fun of such accounts and I don't try to refute them. If that's what Piper says he was seeing and experiencing in those minutes, on what basis would I say, "No, you did not"?

Closer to home, I myself know three individuals who reported on situations that took them to—let's say, other ways of being. I'm not sure if any of the three was considered clinically dead in those moments. One was my mother; when she gave birth to one of my older sisters way too fast, she floated up and looked down on herself on the hospital table. One was a dear friend who, like Piper, was in a horrific vehicle accident; she saw herself and her moped on the side of the road and then headed down a luminous tunnel with beautiful music playing. And the third was my priest, who had had very serious intestinal surgery and felt wrapped in brilliant light. Like Piper, none of them felt scared or wanted to come "back." I guess that does give me some comfort, though I wasn't necessarily searching for comfort about the after-death part. (Like many, including those at our Café mortel, I do feel some trepidation about being in horrific physical pain before I die.)

As you know, Steve, it's almost time for my annual migration to my parents' home and then to Europe. I feel like we've opened up a lot of boxes and wonder which we should try to explore before I'm farther away. I'll be grateful to learn which of the hanging threads, to try out another metaphor, you're most interested in "tying up"—if there is any tying up that can be done on these topics.

Cheers,

i.

Cornish, NH
June 10, 2012

Dear Irene,

The last line of your last missive may say it all by suggesting that there is no tying up to be done. In other words, no certainty to be had, alas. That is what I was getting at when I wrote about being envious of other people's certainty. I wasn't at all disappointed to have you write that you don't have such certainty yourself. We've had enough conversations, though, for me to assume that you have more than I do.

I grew up in a very narrow world. I had no idea of the number of other religions that existed, or the even greater number of religions that were displaced and eradicated over the centuries by more dominant groups. It's clear that those more dominant groups became more dominant, more widespread, through political and military means, not because people who followed, say, Celtic druids or the priests of Zoroaster, thought about it and said, "Oh, yeah, that other religion makes more sense." Now, I look around and see not just many different major religions, but many variations within each of them. Add to those the lesser-known and smaller-scale traditions, often of indigenous peoples, that still exist, and you get a very broad range of beliefs, many of which teach the certainty that they are right and that the others are not. Obviously, they're not all correct.

This little diatribe is by way of explaining again why I can't accept that anybody has the corner on the Truth about God, or about what happens after death. But it wouldn't be accurate to say that I feel bad about not having a strong religious belief, a belief so strong that it feels like knowing. I feel unsettled at times, but I think I embrace the mystery of life and death all the more for that.

I appreciated what you wrote about ritual and its importance, and even the suggestion that my appreciation of ritual when it comes to the end of life might hint at my own deep-down feeling that "all those religions who profess that death is not an absolute end might be onto something." Actually, it's not deep-down at all. I have a pretty strong belief that something is waiting for us after this life. But when I step back from that belief and give it a hard look, I have to admit two things: First, I have no idea what it is that will come next and no way of finding out; and second, my "gut" feeling about an afterlife is heavily influenced by my upbringing in a Catholic family and in a country dominated by Judeo-Christian tradition. And if Judeo-Christianity turns out to be wrong, then I could be wide of the mark, as well.

I think my appreciation of ritual is based in psychology. Rituals can be comforting; they can help with transitions (such as the transition between life with a particular loved one and life without him or her). But ritual as practiced by organized religions often loses me. It starts to feel as though it's more about the institution than the individual. It can feel like a way of investing power in, or keeping power with, religious leaders who lead the rituals. Some time ago, I read a book called *Sacred Dying* by Megory Anderson about creating rituals for ourselves, and for our family and friends, rituals for all of this life's passages, including its last one.[26] That is the image I had in my mind when I read what you wrote about wanting to sit with the body of a just-deceased loved one. To be with that person's body and soul, in love and in grief. That's a ritual I can trust. The idea you mentioned at our Café mortel of a group in any community being ready to step in to care for and prepare a body: That feels like the right idea to me, too.

In the end, certain or uncertain might not be what is important, anyway. We can all believe quite differently with no idea who, if any of us, is right. What is important is what we do with those beliefs while we are here in this world. How do they influence the way we live, the way we treat other people, the way we raise our families and care for those close to us?

And, of course, how do they prepare us to die, suddenly or slowly, painfully or peacefully, alone or embraced? That is what we have been thinking and writing about all these months: Living with an acceptance of our mortality, as though our end could be as near as the next moment, and through that living and acceptance, preparing ourselves for a death that is peaceful, even graceful, for us, and both a lesson and a gift for those close to us. How we live and how we die are so intimately connected, but it's a connection we often lose sight of, isn't it?

Enjoy your summer in Europe. Don't forget to write.

s

La Tour-de-Peilz, Switzerland

4 July 2012

Dear Steve,

I actually arrived here yesterday, but it seemed poetic to wait until today to write, since my records show that we began this exchange exactly one year ago. And what a year it's been! Our exchanges have felt miraculous to me for the freedom we've given ourselves to express any thought, no matter how outrageous or personal, and—having expressed those thoughts no-holds-barred—for the opportunity to grow by changing our minds. I suspect it's going to take me some time to assess the true substance of those changes, so I won't summarize them now. I'm not sure I could even if I wanted to try.

However, it did seem worthwhile to register the fact that we've sustained this for a full year. Our year of life with death, we could call it. It's felt very life-affirming. Still, the year part makes me suspect we should end these exchanges now—though not before expressing profound thanks. I can't think of too many other people I know who would have agreed to try this experiment with me. On second thought: maybe there are more than I realize. Let's try another Café mortel when I'm back in New Hampshire and, as the spirit moves us, stew on how to find other interlocutors for these kinds of conversations.

So, thanks. You and Nora, too, have a great summer!

irene

CHAPTER 7

WHAT ABOUT GRIEF?

Cornish, NH
September 22, 2012

Dear Irene,

Well, I'm back. It turns out that our year or so of frequent and some-times lengthy exchanges didn't exhaust the topics of death, dying, and mortality. Who knew?

We never explored the topic of grief in much depth. It's something I've been thinking about lately. It's something I think about often, in fact, in relation to many of my Hand to Heart clients. I work with these people and their families until shortly—sometimes very shortly—before the death, but I usually have little or no contact with survivors afterward, so I don't get to see how they grieve. I can imagine, though, that how the grieving goes has a lot to do with how the death went, among many other factors.

I was making massage home visits recently with a man who, it turned out, was only a few weeks from his death when I first saw him. He had never had a massage before, as is often the case with Hand to Heart clients. A hospice nurse had suggested it, and his wife called to make that first appointment, so he was a little unsure of what to expect. He loved it, though, and I got to see him several times in his last days. Each time, he was a little weaker, eventually needing to stay in his bed, and then being less and less awake. When I arrived for what clearly would be my last visit with him, his wife met me at the door and said he had had a bad night, with a lot of anxious movements and troubled breathing. She was clearly in as much distress as she believed he was.

She left me alone with him, and I did about forty-five minutes of gentle massage and sitting with still hands resting on him, accompanied by—if I remember correctly—some soft classical music. He quieted quickly and was sleeping peacefully when I left. He died with his family around him seven hours later. His wife wrote a note to me not long afterward: "[His] breathing had eased and was quite quiet, and he was able to fall into a quiet sleep. Such a relief! That continued during the day, no more restlessness. . . . He was so peaceful afterwards. Our hope was that he could stay in his home and pass away peacefully, and that is actually what happened. Early in the evening, he just fell into a deeper sleep and we were all able to be there as he quietly just stopped breathing."

I'm sure that the grieving process for his wife and the rest of his family will be affected by the depth of their relationships and the profound feeling of losing someone whose life might well have seemed an extension of their own. And I assume that that intense grief will last for some time. But I can't help thinking that the immediate period of grief is a little easier because the man's death was peaceful, apparently free of pain and distress.

In a broader sense, following on that logic, being comfortable about the actual dying of a loved one, meaning the mental and spiritual place they were in for their last breaths, must make the grieving period easier. Even as I type it, though, "easier" doesn't sound like the right word. There is nothing easy about it, I realize. Even traditions that seem most accepting of and comfortable with mortality understand that knowing we all will die doesn't make losing someone easy or pain-free, and that supporting people who are grieving is important. In *The Tibetan Book of Living and Dying*, from which I've quoted to you before, Sogyal Rinpoche writes: "A person who is going through bereavement for the first time may simply be shattered by the array of disturbing feelings, of intense sadness, anger, denial, withdrawal, and guilt that they suddenly find are playing havoc inside of them. Helping those who have just gone through the loss of someone close to them will call for all your patience and sensitivity."[1]

But there is one kind of "help" that people close to the bereaved often offer that is no help at all. I'm sure you've seen examples of it, too. It goes something like, "It's been six months (or seven, or a year; pick a number). It's time to move on. Put it behind you." The presumptuousness of such a statement always catches me by surprise. How can anyone know when someone else should essentially turn off their grief? Years ago, I had a massage client, a woman in her seventies, who had recently lost her husband. She had family around and plenty of support, but while she was an active and seemingly happy person, she still felt the loss every day. And then, one day, she came in for her massage and told me that she had just recently, two years after her husband's death, begun to feel as though she was on the other side of her grief. It had never disabled her, but she continued to feel it as long as it was there, and then one day it wasn't. I admired her for such a clearheaded and self-respecting approach to her loss.

To turn once more to Sogyal Rinpoche: "Whatever you do, don't shut off your pain; accept your pain and remain vulnerable. However desperate you become, accept your pain as it is, because it is in fact trying to hand you a priceless gift: the chance of discovering . . . what lies beyond sorrow."[2] Two words from that quotation stand out for me: "remain vulnerable." We often don't do that readily or well, do we? Maybe that's why people are uncomfortable with grief, even other people's grief. It makes clear our vulnerability to pain and loss.

These are scattered thoughts about grief, I know. The topic could lead us in many different directions, such as the grief that takes place in the period before someone dies, and the grief of the dying person himself, to name a couple. You point the way.

Best wishes,

Steve

White Plains, NY
Christmas 2012

Dear Steve,

Hitting Christmas and experiencing the one-year anniversary of my brother-in-law's death reminded me that I had not yet responded to your comments on grief, despite having been moved by them and intending to write back quickly. I guess I was pretty busy trying to stay focused on the day-by-day, especially since this fall afforded my husband and me the chance to be in Switzerland.

What's most present in my mind right now after re-reading what you'd written in the context of my family's loss is your contention that no one should prescribe for someone else the right length of time or intensity of grieving. I mainly agree with that, however, I realize I also admire traditions like Judaism that have quite clear ideas of how to grieve. Sitting shiva, reciting Kaddish, and placing stones on a Jewish grave have made their way into most Americans' consciousness, I think.[3] I'm not sure that the tradition of a specific end to mourning has. There are lots of variations within the branches of Judaism, and even among specific congregations, but most follow three phases of mourning where each is supposed to get less intense: seven days (shiva), thirty days (shloshim), and thirteen months (yud bet hodesh). One detail about shiva that particularly moves me is that the mourners sit on a low stool or the ground. After the Kaddish prayers are said on the seventh day, they are told by visitors to "stand up." Being physically low to the ground seems like a powerful way to honor the excruciating initial grief. One has been knocked down by it, so to speak. And standing up seems like a beautiful symbol for beginning to reenter normal life. Individuals also stand up to say Kaddish at a specific moment in all public services in the ensuing months. (Interesting that one is not supposed to say Kaddish privately.) And then the official mourning period is over at a year. That makes a certain sense to me. I love both the idea of the mourners being honored within the community by visitors

during the seven days of shiva and at a specific point in all religious services (only the mourners stand and say Kaddish at that point). Frankly,
I find just as compelling the idea of "genug shoin" ("enough already"),
even as I would agree with you and your example, that sometimes the
"enough" is more than one year.[4]

We had all hoped that our sister Maria and our nieces would come to be
with us in New York this Christmas—we used to always be a full family at
this holiday until Steve got too sick to travel. The girls especially, however,
really wanted to be at home in London, and Maria agreed to it. When we
talked to them today on the phone, all three of them sounded pretty down.
We didn't try to talk them out of that, of course. But we are also hoping
and praying that they can focus more and more on the present, especially
knowing that they took the best possible care of Steve and that they're all
young with a lot of life ahead of them, my sister included.

I completely get the sadness on the actual anniversary of a death.
I've already shared with you that anniversaries of the Zantops' deaths are
always very hard for me, even though it's been more than ten years now,
and it's by no means the only time I grieve for them. There's something
about the date of a death coming up on the calendar.

So here's "Irene therapy": I don't think I've mentioned to you yet an
amazing passage in one of my favorite novels by Thomas Hardy, *Tess of
the D'Urbervilles*. I'm not saying you have to run out and read it, especially as it is a long one. But perhaps you'll want to look at the passage
I'm thinking of right now. The protagonist, Tess, a young, simple village
girl, is raped by a cavalier, wealthy man who has posed as her benefactor,
securing her employment with his mother, for instance. In the wake of
being raped by the impostor benefactor, returning to her home, bearing a
sickly babe who dies soon after birth, and mourning the child, Tess takes
a rather philosophical turn. Reviewing the major events in her life:

> [She] noted dates as they came past in the revolution of the year; the
> disastrous night of her undoing at Trantridge with its dark background

of The Chase; also the dates of the baby's birth and death; also her own birthday; and every other day individualized by incidents in which she had taken some share. She suddenly thought one afternoon when looking in the glass at her fairness, that there was yet another date, of greater importance to her than those; that of her own death, when all these charms would have disappeared; a day which lay sly and unseen among all the other days of the year, giving no sign or sound when she annually passed over it, but not the less surely there.[5]

There are many aspects of this passage that have stuck with me over the years since I first read it as a teenager, starting with the one I've already mentioned of the power of anniversaries more generally. Surely the most striking is the idea that we will in fact each die on a specific day and that that day is part of the cycle of a year that we live through time after time—at least those of us who are luckier than Tess's infant and others who die young. By having this thought, Tess wraps her mind around her own death in a way we've noted that few young people do (she's about twenty at this point in the novel).

It's the critical next step that interests me, even though it's left unarticulated in this passage. When we take in our inevitable death, I think, we're bound to grieve for ourselves, to think through how one day we just won't be in the world anymore. And such grief seems okay to me, as long as we don't stay stuck there. What I'd forgotten about Tess until rereading this passage recently, is that after her realization and what I'm assuming was a shocked moment of self-grieving—for her future lost beauty, her future death—she actually relaunches *her life*. The narrator summarizes it poetically: "Almost at a leap Tess thus changed from simple girl to complex woman."[6] He then reports on how Tess leaves her parents' home and her natal village, seeking and getting employment—employment she genuinely enjoys—elsewhere.

So, if we're going to talk about grief, we need to include anticipatory grief. And if we're talking anticipatory grief, there's the grief about our own demise as in the passage above, and also the grief we feel in advance of a loved one's death. We felt that kind of grief quite often in Switzerland this summer and fall with regard to my mother-in-law. She turned ninety-eight just before my husband and I left to return to the States, and she didn't even want us to joke about getting to one hundred. She often confided to me that she is more than ready to die, but she's worried that one of her daughters is not ready to lose her. I think she's right about that. Further, my sister-in-law is experiencing a kind of anticipatory grief that expresses itself as mild panic and depression. To get back to one of the points you raised: I don't judge her for that. Those emotions are part of a long and complicated relationship—not necessarily more complicated than other relationships, mind you. Simply unique and intense, as most mother-daughter relationships are.

My own anticipatory grief for my mother-in-law is understandably different. Partly of course because I'm a daughter-in-law, not a daughter, and partly because of my specific set of attitudes that have been shaped by the exchanges you and I have been having and also for sure by what is going on with my father. Which brings me, I think, to another kind of anticipatory grief. For the last several years, my father has not only been developing more and more severe physical problems, he also has been developing increasingly severe dementia. I'm sure you and I have both seen lots of variations on dementia. In terms of my own father, I recognize less and less of the person who raised us. My father speaks less and less. He moves less and less. His eyes are becoming more and more blank. Every once in a while, he comes out with something or makes a gesture that is so familiar from the man we knew for all those decades. Those moments both shock and delight us. But mainly he's becoming a stranger who physically resembles our father. I've registered many times in myself a sadness about losing that man I knew and struggled with, even as I try to be really nice to the one who now lives at the house I grew up in. In fits and starts I am grieving my father while his body—and perhaps more of his personality than he can express—is still present.

Does that make sense?

Whoah. My heart feels really heavy. I'm not sure I should have gone down this path Christmas night. Hope you had some joy at your house.

Yours,

Irene

Cornish, NH

December 28, 2012

Dear Irene,

Yes, Christmas with my granddaughters and other family was a joy. Of course, trash day, or even root-canal day with my granddaughters would be a joy, so there was no surprise there. On the opposite side of the emotional scale, what you report about grieving your father doesn't surprise me either.

One of my favorite short stories is "The Dead," by James Joyce, from his collection of stories called *Dubliners*. (It's also one of my favorite movies, by the way. The last film by the director John Huston, starring his daughter, Anjelica Huston, with the screenplay by her brother, Tony Huston. It also features a gorgeously sad Irish ballad, "The Lass of Aughrim," sung by tenor Frank Patterson. Worth seeing.) The story is an intense and beautifully written portrayal of relationships in turmoil. And it is pervaded by grief. Grief is there in the grim and unpleasant mother of an alcoholic man, who grieves for the man her son did not grow to be. And it fills that man himself, possibly for the same reason and likely for the maternal relationship he lost long ago.

But mostly the story's grief is in the two main characters, Greta and Gabriel. It isn't far into the story that the cracks in their relationship begin to show, especially in her longing for something different between them. Longing for something different can also be seen as grieving for the lack or loss of that something, right?

Grief becomes almost a character in its own right in the last part of the story, when Greta and Gabriel return to their hotel and she breaks down while telling him the story of a boy she'd known when she was young, a boy who loved her and for whom she cared very much. He died young, maybe because he'd come out in the cold rain to see her, even though he was already ill. It was decades ago, and she still carries the grief as a great burden. The story ends with one of the best soliloquies that I know of, as Gabriel looks out the window at the snow "falling softly, softly falling," and assesses his own life, his own failure to ever love a woman the way this young boy had loved the girl who became his own wife, and his own swift movement to the end of his life. Joyce, as Joyce could, makes this heartbreaking scene a thing of absolute beauty, in all its sadness and grief.[7]

If something that I wrote early in these exchanges is true, that we are all suffering and we are all longing for ways to ease our suffering, then it also makes sense that we are all grieving. If loss is pervasive in life, then so is grief.

Which means that advising people in grief to get over it is even more misguided than I was originally thinking. More likely, we don't ever get over grief, but instead learn to live with it. We bring it into our lives and our souls, where it can be a quiet resident or a disruptive one. Losing grief isn't the point. Working with it is. I appreciated what you wrote about the Jewish traditions of mourning that follow someone's death, a great example how important ritual can be in giving structure to our reactions and emotions surrounding life's highs and lows. Mourning and grief can be quite different, though, with the latter sometimes far outlasting the former.

Many of us have a type of practice with loss and grieving, distinct from the deaths of family members or the divorces of parents or the like. That practice comes from our relationships with animals. "We who choose to surround ourselves with lives even more temporary than our own lives within a fragile circle, easily and often breached. . . . We cherish memory as the only certain immortality, never fully understanding the necessary plan." Those words are from an essay called "The Once-Again Prince" by a little-known writer named Irving Townsend, from his collection *Separate Lifetimes*.[8]

I told you a long time back that I didn't have many childhood experiences with death and dying that helped me become comfortable with the topic. That was even more true when it came to the pets we had. We had a German shepherd early on, but not for terribly long. I think her name was Missy, and I remember her as a boisterous, lively dog—perhaps too boisterous and lively for my parents. One day, she was just gone. I don't think any of us four children were told in advance, and we weren't told afterward (or at least I wasn't) exactly what happened. To this day, I don't know. The same thing happened with a cat we briefly had.

We had other pets, including a wonderful beagle named Schmo (I can't explain the name), that we got close to over several years. But he was suddenly gone one day, too, with no details provided that I remember (although I do remember that he hadn't been feeling well). Fast-forward to when my son, Jesse, was growing up and his only sibling was a big, fun-loving golden retriever. At about age ten, Max got cancer, and he died about ten months later. Jesse was in on all of the discussions about Max's health, including when we finally made arrangements for our vet to come to our home to put him down. Jesse was fifteen. He, his mother, and I gave Max a last meal (a cheeseburger), then knelt on the floor beside him and cried as he died. I am thinking specifically of Jesse's experience with this, because while he missed his friend tremendously, he was, I think, aware of and comfortable with the fact that Max needed to go when he did. For the rest of that winter, this teenager who was typically pushing the envelope in many ways, would don a pair of boots every evening and go out to Max's grave to say goodnight. He even wrote about losing Max in his college entrance essay. (He got in.)

The same vet who came to our house that day figures into another story about life, death, and pets. Our next dog was with us for just under fifteen years. Over her last year, she was failing steadily, and when we took her to the vet one day—he had known her since she was a puppy—he could see that she was uncomfortable and having trouble moving about. He also looked in her eyes and told us: "I don't see her in there." It was time. He gave us his home number to call him when we were ready, which we did a couple of days later, a Saturday.

When he arrived at our house, he was accompanied by his two young sons, about seven and eleven years old. The boys played in the yard while we talked, but they were in the doorway of our living room, watching us on the floor with our dog and their father as he inserted the needle. Watching us cry and comfort her and then hold her body. I think many people might have been disturbed by having the children there, but we trust this vet completely and so were inclined to see it in a different light. When I talked to him about it later, he told me that they went with him on house calls often and had seen many animals die. He thought it was good for them, and even suggested that it had helped them deal with the recent death of a grandmother. I don't doubt that he was right.

As I write this, what is becoming clear again is not that understanding and accepting death necessarily makes losing someone close to you, whether person or pet, easy. The grief will be there. But in some way that I'm having trouble articulating, accepting mortality must make it more tolerable, perhaps because of what we wrote about a while ago: that when you don't see death (yours or someone else's) as something being done to you, you might have an easier time incorporating the loss into your life and, as they say, moving on.

You mentioned anticipatory grief, which is one of the topics I was hoping we would discuss. I said earlier that I don't usually get to see family members of my clients grieve, but I was talking only about the grief that comes after a death. I see an awful lot of people who are watching a loved one approach the end, and I know that for many or most people, the letting go and the grief begin long before the death.

Another kind of anticipatory grief that comes to mind could be given the complicated-sounding name of "vicarious anticipatory grief," I guess. I'm thinking of the pain that a dying person might feel because of the grief and suffering that his or her family and friends will feel after that person is gone. It's related to people's wish not to be a burden on loved ones, I imagine. Just as you don't want to be a burden as you are dying, you don't want to be one afterward, and you can anticipate the grief of those who love you.

Here is a story from my Hand to Heart experience that comes to mind now. It's a bit long, but it's a good one, so bear with it.

My client Sue lived with active cancer in her body for most of twenty years. She had multiple surgeries. There were many years in which she received the poison of chemotherapy more months than she did not. She had pain, especially in her last few years. She eventually developed a tumor in her upper chest that broke through her skin, becoming a foul and festering wound. Every time she was given a choice between ending treatment—thereby allowing the disease to take its course and her life—and continuing with her suffering, she chose to continue. The fragility and the preciousness of life were two sides of the same coin to her, and she held it tightly in her fist until the end.

I began doing massage with Sue many years before she died. I met her because she was part of a breast-cancer support group that my wife facilitated through her job at a local hospital. She would come to my home for massages occasionally, and because she didn't have much money, I didn't charge her. Sometimes, I would find a five-dollar bill or a bag of cookies on the massage table after she left. She would never call me for an appointment, because she couldn't ask for that kind of help, but she accepted whenever I called her.

John O'Donohue, whom I've quoted in several of our exchanges, often wrote about the importance of "thresholds" in life, and I have come to understand that when someone is given a long approach to death, a decline over many months or years, there will be many thresholds to cross. Accepting that your life is no longer the boundless territory it once seemed is one. For Sue, one of the biggest thresholds was accepting that she could no longer do everything for herself, and that she needed to allow others to help. I know that she grieved that loss of independence. It was a huge step for her to allow former coworkers to contribute money so that her health insurance could continue. In our relationship, that threshold was allowing me to come to her home to give her massages to save her the difficulty of driving to me, and I did that for the last couple of years of her life.

I would lug my table up the stairs of her split-level home and set it up in her living room. For a long time, she was able to get onto the table herself and was comfortable lying on it for the length of the massage. When she was going through chemo treatments, she sometimes barely had the strength for it, but she would get herself up there because she felt the massages were important. Toward the end, we used a massage chair instead, because she couldn't lie comfortably on the table, and because we could position her so there was less pain from the tumor in her chest. She was using oxygen at home and often didn't have the strength to talk. For the last year or so, because of damage to a nerve, she had no voice but a whisper. The tumor grew in spite of every effort to arrest it. It seeped blood, and she was usually anemic. Sometimes, her skin seemed transparent to me; I felt I could almost see through her.

It was only in the last year or two of her life that she would make direct references to the likelihood she would die of her disease, and only in the last few months that those references became frequent and more certain. Still, as her body became more and more insubstantial and her awareness of her nearing end more acute, her spirit remained strong. "Will to live" has become too stale a term for what I saw in Sue. It was simply her intention to be here every possible minute.

I wondered sometimes why she would put herself through all of that. Many people I've talked with as they approached death, and many others who watched a loved one on that approach, have said they would never willingly experience that kind of suffering. They would allow the disease to take them rather than put themselves or their families through it. But the concept of "a good death" is easily oversimplified, and when simplified, it can seem to be a template for how someone *should* approach death: if there is a good death, then there is also a bad death. If there is dying well, there must also be dying badly.

Of course, it's not that simple, and there is no template. Even as I wondered, I knew at least part of why Sue would not allow her own suffering to end: She was thinking of her two grandchildren. They lived two hours away, and it was not until the later stages of her illness that she stopped driving over to see them on weekends, just to be with them, and so they could be with her. She hated the idea of them not having her in their lives, and she wouldn't let that happen any sooner than was necessary. In the end—because she saw so much less of them over the last weeks—it seemed to me that she wasn't remaining alive so she could have more time with them as much as she was remaining alive just to be on the same planet with them for another day or hour. The longer she was here, the longer they had her in their lives. She was anticipating the grief they would feel when she died, and she wanted to delay that as long as possible. It wasn't only her own life that she knew to be fragile and precious.

One morning, Sue woke up to see that she was bleeding from the open tumor on her chest. It had invaded a blood vessel, and she was hemorrhaging. She was rushed to her local hospital, then transferred to Dartmouth-Hitchcock Medical Center. A doctor told her there was little they could do. He told her and her family that it seemed the end had finally come. The only, and very slight, hope involved immediate surgery to try to seal the leaking artery. But it was risky, it wouldn't change the progression of her disease, and she was so weak that he estimated perhaps a 10 percent chance she would survive the operation.

She took the chance. The surgery was begun and shortly into it, Sue died.

I had seen enough of Sue to say this much: It would be simplistic to fault her choices because they caused her "unnecessary" suffering. The power of the grief she felt for all of her own losses while she was sick was one thing, but it didn't outweigh her vicarious anticipatory grief, her sense of the great pain that she wanted to forestall for her grandchildren and the rest of her family.

S.

Lebanon, NH
19 March 2013

Dear Steve,

Your phrase "vicarious anticipatory grief" and your illustration of it through your client Sue have moved me deeply. The phenomenon makes perfect sense to me and covers the situation I wrote to you about my mother-in-law seeming to keep herself alive at least in part because she didn't want to cause grief to her younger daughter, who didn't seem ready to lose her. But I guess with a severe-enough cancer or reaching an old-enough age, even the strongest will to not cause others pain can't fight off death.

My mother-in-law, Mireille, passed away on February 27.

Between going to the funeral in Switzerland, rushing back to finish up the academic term in New Hampshire, and yesterday starting the spiritual exercise we call Lent, I haven't had much of a chance to process the reality of her death. With you as my interlocutor, I'm going to give it a try.

Needless to say, I am still mourning what happened. Not Mireille's inevitable death, mind you, though I do miss her already. No, I'm sad about what seemed to me to be—at the time of her dying and still now— the avoidable suffering she experienced at the end, despite the best intentions of every family caretaker involved, including me and my attempts to apply what I've been learning these last years from our exchanges and from reading so much about end-of-life issues.

Mireille mainly lived a great life as far as I could tell: she had had a long, happy marriage to a man who adored her; she bore three children, who doted on her from their births to her death; she lived in one of the most beautiful places on Earth, knew that, and treasured her good fortune. But she lived past the point of being happy to be alive. (You might recall me wondering long ago if that would be one of the consequences of her having received a pacemaker.) It's hard to be sure about what sapped her passionate love of life. After chewing it over for a long time—both as I was noticing it diminish and in the weeks since her death—I think there were two main contributing factors.

For one thing, even though she recovered considerably from the major stroke she had had in 2004, regaining her ability to use her right arm and leg and her ability to speak, she never made peace with her new limitations. I think she experienced not feeling stable enough to walk outdoors on her own as a huge deprivation, for example, even though her daughters were faithful and creative about taking her out, at first holding her arm, then watching over her ambulation with the walker, and eventually by pushing her in the wheelchair.

The other factor, I'm convinced, was inadequate treatment of her pain. Like many poststroke victims and many individuals who reach her age, she had both chronic and acute pains. If she didn't receive her pain medication at just the right time as her almost-constant headaches were intensifying, they got so bad that she would retreat to her bed in a wicked mood. Most serious of the intermittent problems were clots that would make her limbs swell, causing her excruciating pain.

The result of all this was that she was less and less able to register pleasure with the aspects of daily life that were still available to her. She loved well-prepared food and dinner conversation, for instance, but increasingly she refused to join us at the table, sometimes citing her headaches and sometimes giving no reason. In the last couple of years, she seemed to get impatient with any of our attempts at storytelling. Jokes, recitals of odd social incidents, reports on beautiful birds or flowers spotted by one of us got shorter and shorter under her glare or indifference.

Mireille had a very cooperative, patient primary-care physician. Still, as you observed once, training in palliative care has only very recently become part of standard medical training here, as in Switzerland, and he is an older doctor. As a result of finally reading that marvelously helpful book you lent me, *Handbook for Mortals*, I got bolder in querying whether she was getting adequate pain relief.[9] I was politely ignored and once met with a statement I've heard from my father's doctor, too: "We're not there yet." Not where yet? And when do we get there?! I find refusal to prescribe stronger meds hard to accept in the context of an elderly—in my mother-in-law's case, *very* elderly—individual in pain who sometimes expresses the desire not to be alive anymore. Unlike my brother-in-law, Steve, for instance, it wasn't like Mireille had any serious business she had to be clearheaded about. Then, too, the pain itself was making her unable to interact with those around her. I was not talking physician-assisted suicide; I just wanted her to get more pain relief. I find concern about the potential risk of addiction in such cases ridiculous.

More and more troubled by what I saw as inadequate treatment of her pain, I tried one nonmedical technique from another book you'd given me. In *Who Dies?* Stephen Levine talks about "softening around the pain," which he explains as: "Not trying to change the pain, but letting it float free, letting it just be there in space, not even trying to get rid of it."[10] To achieve that attitude, he suggests conducting an investigation of the pain. Well, that's just what I decided to do with my mother-in-law one day when she started complaining to me about how uncomfortable she was. I asked her to tell me more about what the pain felt like: Where was it exactly? Did it feel hot or cold? Did it move around or stay put? Did it go deep or seem to be on the surface? Did it throb or ache? Did it seem to have a color or a texture? I don't know if it was her surprise at the genuine interest I expressed or at the nature of my query, but we discussed the pain she was feeling for more than fifteen minutes. I also don't know if this exchange calmed her because I was simply distracting her from the pain or if describing the pain allowed her to develop a different relationship to it à la Levine. I doubt it matters, but it was gratifying to feel like I'd been able to help her momentarily.

Unfortunately, such moments were just blips in the saga of Mireille's suffering. One Saturday night in February, a few months after my husband and I had returned to the States, another clot formed in her leg, and she found herself once again in terrific pain. Her daughters and son-in-law took her to the emergency room of the major hospital in Lausanne, where a difficult discussion ensued about surgical removal of the clot. She opted for it. The surgeon asked about her wishes for resuscitation if something went wrong during the surgery, and she vehemently expressed the wish that nothing be done to revive her. The surgery went extremely well, though, and the pain was gone. She was feeling so much better in the immediate aftermath of the surgery that she even enjoyed a visit from a young person she didn't know that well (the pregnant wife of her daughter's godson). This was the Mireille I knew and loved: someone who rejoiced in all forms of life, especially of young and new life.

Alas, that phase didn't last long either. Just days later, she was transferred to the regional hospital closer to her home, and she started to go downhill very rapidly. She found herself experiencing terrible pain again. The morphine she was given at that stage seemed to make her skin so sensitive that she couldn't be touched, so it was discontinued. It's still not clear to me today if alternate pain medications were tried, but if they were, they didn't seem to help much. We children agreed at least implicitly—I don't recall the words being said out loud—that she was dying. What we did say to each other and to the hospital staff was that she wanted to die at home, but the staff replied that she was too frail to move. Indeed, she screamed even when the nurses tried to reposition her in the hospital bed. As if being in the hospital was not miserable enough, her hospital room faced an ugly concrete wall, so my sisters-in-law opted to keep the curtains drawn, making the setting depressingly dark—but better than staring at that ugly wall.

We were in phone contact with my sisters-in-law several times a day. I could hear loudly in my head my own sister Maria's advice for years now: don't second-guess the caregivers on the ground. Be as supportive as you possibly can be. And I believe we were. Not just we in the States to my worried sisters-in-law in Switzerland, but also with each other. Philippe and I rose to a new level of cooperation and understanding with one another about what was going on. It was almost as if one of us just had to start to say something and the other immediately could finish the thought because s/he agreed with it. Even then, in the midst of emergency decision-making, I recognized this harmony and gentleness as the fruit of all our conversations about Mireille's situation, about what we wanted for ourselves, and more generally about end of life.

When my sisters-in-law reported that Mireille was refusing to eat or drink, I looked at Philippe and he looked back, and we mouthed to each other: time to get on a plane. I booked the ticket for Philippe while he started to pack. I had already had to swallow the bitter pill that with my courses at the college in their last week, I would have to wait until she had actually died to justify my departure. So I did what I could: I wrote my good-bye to Mireille, and Philippe promised he would read it to her.

I'd been living for so long with the reality of losing this person I loved, that I didn't need any guidelines from anybody else about what to write— though I hope you're pleased to learn I had read Ira Byock's books since you first mentioned him.[11] I thanked her for accepting me so fully into the family; I thanked her, too, for all the amazing experiences and talks we'd had over the years; I expressed regret for the things we'd hoped to do together and had never managed; I expressed my profound sadness and acknowledged hers for the absence of the next generation of the family that I had hoped to produce; I shared my prayer that she was not currently in pain; and I assured her that the Lord had a plan, even if neither she nor I was privy to exactly how it was going to go from here.

We were enormously grateful—happy, even—that Philippe arrived in Switzerland in time to see his mother and that she was still conscious enough to recognize him. Although the other members of our family are not religious, we were all profoundly relieved when a pastor found her way to Mireille's hospital bed several days after we'd made this request:

Pastor Daisy connected with Mireille immediately over their mutual love of the Swiss Alps. The palliative-care team finally showed up, too.

Still, the gaps in care continued to be profound and consequential up to her very end. No one advised my husband and his sisters about the active dying phase. On what turned out to be the critical last day, the sisters sent Philippe home for a break. Moments later, my mother-in-law started to breathe even more loudly (in the manner referred to as the "death rattle"), and, assuming that she was in pain, one of them ran to get help. She got back just in time to witness the moment of death, but one of her children, her oldest child and only son, was absent. Did that make a difference to Mireille? We'll never know. But it did cause anguish to her kids. And from the larger perspective you and I have been trying to take, it's clear that it was completely avoidable. If only the professional staff had paid more attention to Mireille's dying, they could have communicated to her children what their experience must have told them: she was likely to die soon, and, no, those sounds she was making did not indicate that she was in pain.

Still, we have so much to be thankful for. Mireille's body was taken to her beloved "chambre rose" (her pink bedroom); that is to say, she did get to go home in a manner of speaking. She was not embalmed, but rather ice (changed regularly by the team from the funeral home) and the open windows and February temperatures preserved her just fine for several days, while, among other things, I could arrive from the States, and the local church could accommodate her funeral. Thus, I did spend time with her corpse. I could address her, stroke her hair, hold her hand, pray. I could say good-bye "in person" properly. I know having her body again in her apartment also helped my sisters-in-law make the difficult transition they had been dreading for a long time: from being close to their mother their entire lives to now having to live without her. As with so many aspects of dying we've taken up, Steve, I don't think someone else's death can be fully absorbed the moment you learn of the fact; so while some people might think it bizarre to have a corpse in the apartment for five days, we were grateful.

You've spoken about creating one's own end-of-life rituals that make sense to the individuals involved. Well, it was a gray, cold day for the funeral, but the same pastor who had comforted Mireille and given her communion shortly before her death set an energetic tone in the church that seemed just right. My jazz-loving husband followed up on a request his mother had made while still well to have Olivier, a jazz drummer friend of Philippe's whom my mother-in-law adored, play some numbers with a saxophonist; I think those in attendance were both surprised and thrilled at this unusual twist on funeral protocol. Focusing my eulogy on Mireille's extraordinary love of life rather than on her long and difficult end and lots of practicing out loud beforehand helped me get through my remarks without crying. We held the reception in our little Swiss apartment, where the atmosphere could be personal and cozy. I had to return to the States the day after the funeral because of exam period. Still, I felt so deeply grateful for having been able to say good-bye at least in a certain manner to my mother-in-law and to spend at least a bit of time with the family and others who had known her and loved her. I think that's an element of grieving we should point to explicitly: It helps a lot to be able to be in the company of others who are also mourning. Back to one of the wonderful aspects of the Jewish tradition of sitting shiva and praying for the dead: You do it in community.

To return to one of your initial points about grieving, I do agree that how someone actually dies can affect one's mourning. I still feel the pain Mireille experienced so close to her mortal end like a black cloud hanging over us. But my fervent hope is that one day that cloud will dissipate, and we will spend more and more time thinking about her long and mainly happy life and the great experiences and conversations we had with her.

(Apropos one of the points in your last letter: I realize that some thinkers distinguish carefully between mourning and grieving; but I'll admit to being like most English speakers in mainly using them as synonyms.)

Steve, when I first wrote to you in July 2011 of the three very ill members of my family, it was my father I believed to be closest to death. So it comes as a bit of a shock to realize that, almost two years later, he is the only one of the three still alive. He's had a lot of ups and downs since the days in the nursing home. The "ups" last shorter and shorter. Still, my mother has managed to keep her promise to him, and he is being taken care of in his own home. He'll turn eighty-four if he makes it to December, an older age than his parents, grandparents, or two younger brothers reached. Like Mireille, though in different ways because of his dementia, he mostly lets us know that he's not very happy to be alive. Then again, there are occasional meals when he swallows his food with relish.

Every time our phone rings, I think to myself that it could be news of Dad's passing. As much as I feel a little squeeze on my heart at the sound of that ring, I'm not afraid or panicked. I know that I've been living my relationship to him as fully as the circumstances of both his health and my life allow. I've already forgiven him for the grief he caused me when I was younger, and I've asked his forgiveness for things I've done or said that must have hurt him. I tell him I love him every time I see him. Several weeks ago, a bunch of us siblings—five of the six—were home at the same time, and we showered him with attention. A few days after our departure, he asked my mother where those nice people had gone.

What do you think? Is being able to smile at that a sign that I have already mourned the father who's gone and fallen in love with the man who took his place?

Irene

Cornish, NH
March 22, 2013

Dear Irene,

Thank you for the news about your mother-in-law, and for the way you told the story. I can't help thinking that the two stories we exchanged in these last writings epitomize not just what we feel about grief but also what we've been trying to get at with all of this musing, philosophizing, soul-searching, and storytelling that we've been doing for a couple of years now.

Three quick thoughts in reaction to what you wrote.

One: You expressed the hope that your memories of Mireille eventually will be of her as she was for the many years you knew her before her difficult dying. I think that will be the case. I have heard it many times: The images of end-of-life suffering fade; the images of life replace them.

Two (and I know we've both said this often): While embracing our mortality has its benefits, making dying and grieving easy is not among them. More endurable, perhaps, for having had a place prepared for them in our minds. But never easy.

Three: Your thoughts about your father are really wonderful to read. Numbers 1 and 2 above will serve you well.

Steve

CHAPTER 8

WHAT'S SO GREAT ABOUT MORTALITY ANYWAY?

Cornish, NH
July 8, 2013

Dear Irene,

You and I have covered a lot of ground in the e-mailed conversation we've been conducting over these last years. Thanks to my job, I continue to do a lot of thinking about death and dying, but our written exchanges and the face-to-face conversations we've been having sporadically since we met have made me broaden that thinking. Or maybe organize it a little more than it had been. What we each wrote about the justice or injustice of dying, and about caregiving, for example, took those areas of thought to places I hadn't fully expressed to myself. So this conversation and our relationship, whatever else they lead to, have had at least that great benefit.

I am just coming off a week of having my two granddaughters, two and four years old, here with us, an experience that is always joyful and exhausting. They are happy and active kids who live from moment to moment, at times content and at times complaining, but not thinking much about what will happen tomorrow or the next day, except for the vague notion that a reunion with their parents is going to come on one of those tomorrows.

It's interesting that while I'm trying to bring my own attention to each moment, and to stop worrying as much as I usually do about tomorrows, I'm trying to get the girls to take a bit more of the long view. *You already*

183

had ice cream today, so you'll have to wait until tomorrow. You can't ride horses here because we don't have horses, so you will have to wait several days until you're back with Mom. Not now, later. Not today, tomorrow. I almost think that I need to be careful not to push their attention entirely into the future, at the cost of losing the importance of this very moment, this breath they are taking right now.

It reminds me of the lesson I got when I did a home-visit massage with a good friend who had advancing dementia. When our session was over, he was writing a check to me and asked me what day it was. I wasn't thinking clearly when I said, "The Twenty-Second." He wrote that down, and then said, "And the month?" I felt foolish for not anticipating that, and replied, "Oh, sorry. May. It's May Twenty-Second." He wrote that down. Without looking up or taking his pen away, he asked, "And the year?"

His disease had cut the cord that had kept him—that keeps all of us—tethered to our place in time. My friend did not exist in a world of yesterday, today, and tomorrow. He was living in a sort of floating now. In a way, that's the ideal that many spiritual teachers are encouraging: live in the moment. But my friend has been forced into that situation, with much loss in the process, whereas true enlightenment would mean awareness of the past and the future, and choosing to live in the moment.

I find myself wondering, why is that important, exactly?

There seems no way to avoid thinking of what is ahead. That, after all, is at the core of what we have been getting at. If we embrace our mortality, we get to ask the ultimate looking-ahead question: How do we want to die? And the related question: How do I want to live the rest of my life?

A few years ago, when I was at that intensive Buddhist-based training in New Mexico I've told you about, on being with people who are dying, we were given an exercise that asked a variation of that first question several times in different contexts. At first we were asked to visualize ourselves on our deathbeds at a time many years out—say, twenty or twenty-five years. Who is with us? Where are we? Imagine the scene in detail. For me, that would mean thinking about who in my life today would still be with me, and what they might look like. My granddaughters would be adults, maybe married, maybe mothers. Eek. Now repeat the exercise again, but with the time many years closer. Ten years. Picture everything.

Do it again, only now the time is just one year off. Play the scene out in your mind.

And then do it once more, except the time is now.

If you fully contemplate each step of this exercise, it becomes a powerful way to bring your attention to the reality that you will die someday, and also maybe to the question of how you would want it to happen, should you be given any choice in the matter.

When I think of how I would want to die, I can't help but think of the many people I have watched as they approached death. There are stories among them that I would consider appropriating for myself, with little changes here and there, of course.

One story in particular from the last few months left an indelible mark on me. When Pat was referred to Hand to Heart by her nurse practitioner, I was told that she would likely die soon, and she was very anxious about that. "I don't think this is going to go well," was what the nurse wrote in an e-mail. And in fact, Pat *was* nervous the first time I carried my table up to her small, second-floor apartment. She clearly didn't know what to expect from this large, strange man standing before her when she opened her door, but she was trying to be open-minded, and that openness allowed a strong connection to develop between us over the next several weeks. By only the second and third visits, she was more relaxed, and it was obvious to me that she was getting a significant benefit from the massage sessions.

We talked a little about her life, about music (she was a pianist), but nothing very deep at first. Over time, though, our conversations turned more toward her feelings about what was happening to her. She didn't like it, and she certainly wasn't embracing it in the first weeks I was seeing her.

She had a very large tumor at the base of her neck, which was causing some pain and shortness of breath. She tried a course of radiation to shrink it, but with no benefit. She got weaker and sadder, and yet was always very glad to hear that I was planning to stop by, which I did more and more often. We had some wonderful talks.

Eventually, Pat was unable to get onto the massage table without my help. I would get her positioned, help her out of her clothes, cover her up, and begin the session. She often cried a little as she relaxed, letting go of some of what she was trying to hold back around other visitors. Once, I recited a beautiful John O'Donohue blessing to her, one that ends: "And so may a slow wind work these words of love around you, an invisible cloak to mind your life."[1] She cried and said nothing more than thank you.

One day when I arrived, Pat's eighty-year-old sister-in-law answered the door (there was always someone with her and providing care over her last weeks) and told me that Pat thought she really needed a bath and would understand if I didn't have time to wait (which, in fact, I didn't). "She's in the kitchen if you want to talk to her." Pat was sitting in a chair in the middle of the room, slumped forward because she was too weak to sit up straight. I sat next to her and put my hand on her leg. She told me she hadn't been bathed in a few days and didn't want a massage in that state. I asked if it wouldn't make more sense to have the bath afterward, so she could wash the oil from her skin and hair. She said again that she was too dirty. When I pushed just a little more, she said, "I reek."

"I'm not picking that up," I said, but added that it was entirely up to her.

After a moment, she said: "I'd rather have the massage than not." So I helped her to the room where I set up the table, picked her up and put her onto it, and gave her the massage.

Can you imagine the vulnerability of a proud woman allowing a man she'd known only for a short time to see and be near her when she felt she was unclean? And the grace needed to embrace that vulnerability? I am still amazed by her willingness to allow me to do that massage, to let down her guard and see the moment for what it could be. The importance of accepting compassion and help from another is one of the most touching and important lessons I've gained from Hand to Heart. It's what I hope for my stubborn self when my time comes.

I worked with Pat several more times, the last few with her remaining on a sofa. She couldn't talk much beyond mouthing her words, so we worked in quiet for the most part. I recited the O'Donohue blessing once more. When I was getting ready to leave one time, she held my arm and mouthed "Don't go." I stayed a bit longer. She sometimes wanted to be pulled up into a sitting position, probably to make her back feel better, and when she was up, she would lean into me and hold one of my arms to her chest while I massaged her back with the other hand. When I lowered her back down, she moved my hand to her heart and held it there.

The last time I saw her, while she was sitting up, she lifted her head and looked me in the eye with as clear a gaze as I'd seen from her in a long time. "I'm so fond of you," she whispered.

"I feel the same way," I told her. She died less than twenty-four hours later. I got a call from one of her caregivers just as I was about to leave my office to go see her. She died peacefully, in the company of a few people who loved her. For a death that wasn't likely to go well, one that Pat would have preferred not happen at all for many years to come, I can't imagine it being better.

In his 2012 book, *Immortality: The Quest to Live Forever and How It Drives Civilization*, Stephen Cave made his case that every civilization in human history has been built around trying to outwit mortality.[2] It has been attempted in every way imaginable, he writes, from actual efforts to find an elixir that defied death to spiritual traditions built on the idea of everlasting life.

And all of these efforts fly in the face of, or at least strongly resist, the most fundamental truth about life. It ends. Everything about that truth shapes our lives. The rhythms of a human life are defined by the fact that it has a beginning and an end. We may not know when that end will come, but we know for certain that it will. Our relationships, our careers, and our self-images are all defined by the fact that time is limited.

So what is the lesson here? Embracing mortality must do more than affect the way we die. It's about how we live. If I can bring the importance of each moment to each moment I live, if I can bring the intention of compassion to each relationship in my life, then I might see the most important benefit of accepting death as part of life. I might not just get to die a peaceful and meaningful death. I might get to live a more peaceful and meaningful life. That would be the gift of mortality.

s.

La Tour-de-Peilz
13 July 2013

Dear Steve,

It's a beautiful summer day on Lake Geneva. The sun is shining. The birds are chirping. The mountains across the way have a few clouds perching on them. The sky is a pale, summer-hot blue. And here I am reading your thoughts on "death" once more. Only I don't experience it in the way that might sound. Everything about our exchange has been life-enhancing for me. I think you're right that we should try to ask ourselves: Why?

Part of my answer to that, at least at this point in time, comes from your sharing about your client Pat. It seems to me that when Pat was able to accept that she was dying, she became freed up to register what was going on for her at that very moment, letting go of inherited ideas about what we should fear or what is appropriate or inappropriate. In registering her "present," she was then able to make life-affirming decisions. She let herself have the massage that was available to her right then, even if she hadn't bathed. She let herself grow close to you, someone who was trying to help her, but whom by some people's criteria, anyway, she didn't actually know that well. She even let herself express out loud her fondness for you. A good death, as you write, but maybe more to the point: a good life, no?

I love your rumination about teaching your grandchildren about time. And I feel like I understand your worry that in teaching them to be patient, you might be conditioning them away from living in the moment—something children do so well. I can also relate to your concern for your granddaughters—and all of us—to develop some kind of balance between knowledge of their past, living in the present, and preparing for the future. I hear so often an inner call to get that balance "right," and yet the very ubiquity of the calling makes me suspect I never will. In all humility then, I offer you and our exchange this bumbling response to the call of the present, deeply hoping that others have gotten or will get to a similar response in a different way from the way I got there.

One of the first changes I consciously registered in myself after the Zantops were killed was the attitude that I need to be ready to die at any moment. Given that, especially initially, my friends and I had no idea why the Zantops had been killed, the killers were on the loose, and my own profile as well as that of most of my friends was very similar to theirs, it makes a certain amount of sense that we thought we could be the next target. Still, the attitude I developed and still have has more to do with the swiftness of their deaths. One moment they were home, making lunch, and the next moment they were no longer alive. The particular manner of their deaths also preoccupied me. Will I be numb with fear, or will I be able to pray in my last moments? Will I fight, or will I be still? If my death is not sudden and, rather, I get sick or simply very old and weak, will I become depressed or accept my physical state? This could sound morbid, but I don't experience it that way. Like you, I experience my running through various scenarios as realistic and helpful preparation for the inevitable—not an inevitably violent or tragic death, which, statistically speaking, I'm unlikely to have—but simply an inevitable last moment of my life.

Frequently in the wake of Susanne and Half's murders and still today I ask myself about the present moment: Is it a good one? Such thoughts have led me to be vigilant about attending to relationships; if in the next moment my life is over, I want to leave as much felicity behind as possible. Similarly, I try to take any unpleasant situation I might be in and discover some beautiful or positive aspect of it, because, again, if this is going to be my last or penultimate moment in this world, I don't want to have spent it in frustration, annoyance, or anger. This attitude fits well, I suppose, with my transformed sense of the future.

I became (and mostly remain) incapable of thinking that I know anything about the future. Losing Susanne and Half the way we did made it so incontestable to me that one simply cannot know what is going to happen next. On the most mundane level, I recall having essentially every hour of that last weekend in January 2001 scheduled with activities from Friday morning to late Monday night. I distinctly remember running through the list in my head on Thursday evening: (Friday) teaching, tennis, grocery shopping, dinner with Philippe; (Saturday) house-hunting, quiet evening at home; (Sunday) church, a birthday brunch, a Super Bowl party; (Monday) a mammogram, lunch with a younger faculty member, a television show. I felt determined to keep that rush of activities low-stress, but it didn't occur to me for one second that things wouldn't unfold approximately as planned.

Well, that Saturday-night phone call from my colleague announcing that the Zantops had been killed canceled not only all plans but also the idea of planning itself.

Admittedly, I've been back to making lists of things to do for a while now, but each list carries an invisible, insistent proviso—"if I'm around."

When the reality sunk in that Susanne and Half truly were dead, I also came to realize how much my sense of the longer-term future had vanished. There are the specific ways in which whatever sense I had had of the shape of the rest of my life was wrapped up with them personally because of the deep friendship I had with each of them and the close professional association I had with Susanne. But there was also a way that registering evil intent and murder as present locally led to a transformation of my sense that I will live out my life and the world will go on after me. I no longer remember at what stage the thought crystalized, but at some point I realized that this "new" feeling was actually not new but a reemergence of my conviction as a child during the Cold War that nuclear war could make my whole world disappear in an instant. Somehow there had been a luminous, hopeful phase in between.

So, dear friend, here is another gift of our exchange, of our hard work of trying to let ourselves think through mortality. The present has come to feel like enough. The luminosity is back, though maybe it's light of a different quality. I've written to you before that if I have to die later today or tomorrow, I feel pretty certain it will be okay. Like so many of your clients you've shared about, I suspect I'll feel sad to be losing relationships with people I've come to love so much, but I strongly hope to focus on gratitude in my dying moments, gratitude for having felt alive while I was alive. If the worst part of losing Susanne and Half was a numbness so profound that hours could pass without me registering a damn thing, one of the most comforting aspects was coming out of that stupor and remembering how fully they had lived their lives while they were alive and deciding that I wanted to try to do the same. I knew that that was what they had always wanted for me and all those whom they loved—and they loved a lot of people!

Think of the past? Yes. Remind myself of lessons learned, people loved, promises made. Think of the future? Yes. Rehearse in my mind what I want to do if I get the chance to say good-bye, if I contract an incurable disease, if I realize I am dying. The present? Yes, that's actually all I've got. Those thoughts of past or future only come into being in the present. (I guess that's how I interpret that Rilke line you once quoted to me about learning to see: "all things enter more deeply into me."[3]) Immortality? For me it's having my head and heart in the right place right now. The rest is completely out of my control.

This present moment? Time to get some fresh air and something to eat.

Be well, dear friend,

i.

Cornish, NH
August 18, 2013

Dear Irene,

I feel as though I am overflowing with stories to tell about people I have met through my work, stories that give life and dimension to so much of what we've been discussing. You will remember (maybe not; it was a long time ago) me discussing my client with kidney disease, the one who had doubts about whether to go through with a kidney transplant, with one of her sons providing the kidney. She was filled with worry about whether it was a good idea to allow her son to make the donation, and about whether having the operation would improve her longevity or quality of life enough to be worthwhile.

She did have the transplant, and while she might have lived longer because of it than she would have otherwise, things didn't go particularly well. The new kidney showed signs of her old disease rather quickly. She went on medications intended to slow the progression, but suffered a lot of side effects and setbacks. Eventually, she needed to decide whether to go on dialysis, the only way she could avoid dying. She and her husband talked it through, and she agreed to do it. But what should have been a routine procedure to kill off the donated kidney before she could begin dialysis went badly, and she came out of it with no use of her legs.

She spent many weeks in a rehab hospital in Boston—in an ambulance on the way there, she told me, she was asking herself, "What am I doing here?"—eventually returning home with no significant improvement in her legs. She and her husband tried to settle into the difficult routine of him moving her into the car three times a week to travel the half hour or so to the dialysis center, spending several hours there, then getting her back into the car for the trip home. Between the time and her exhaustion, it typically shot most of a day. She got weaker, suffered incontinence, and had extreme pain in her legs. They hired someone to come in and help her husband care for her a few hours most days.

The time came, after several days in the hospital trying to address an acute problem that had developed, when she said, "Enough." She ended treatment, enlisted the services of a hospice program, and went home. I visited her there the day after she got back; she'd been told she would likely die within a week or so. As I gave her a massage in her bed, she told me about finally reaching the point of letting go. "It's gotten ahead of us," she said, meaning the everyday challenge for her and her husband. "I think we've done as well as we possibly could have, but it's gotten too hard." She worried about her husband's health as he cared for her, moved her, carried her. "I see his body breaking down."

I reminded her that two years earlier, when she was facing the transplant, she was saying such things as "I don't know if I should go through with it"; "I'm not sure I want to make the effort anymore"; and "I don't know if I should let my son give me a kidney." Now, I said to her, everything you're saying is about "we" and "us." She and her husband had arrived at that point after a terribly difficult process, but they had arrived together. Her husband had told me that people sometimes asked how she was doing or why she was continuing to get treatment, and she would say: "It's not good. But I'm alive, and we're together. It's okay." Until they both knew it wasn't.

When I was packing to go, she looked at me and said, "Well, Steve, it's been quite a journey." I agreed and said I was glad to have shared it with her. I saw her once more, a few days later. She was in a deep sleep most of the time I was with her that day, barely opening her eyes when I said hello. I spent an hour with my hands on her. She died the next morning, surrounded by her husband, her kids, and a small crowd of family and others who loved her, each of them now carrying part of her on their own journeys, each given the gift of witnessing her life and her death.

S.

Lebanon, NH

27 January 2014

Dear Steve,

Sorry I didn't manage a New Year's greeting or a response to the beautiful story about your client with kidney disease. Of course I remember you telling me about her; she left a real impression on me! I was happy to learn that she and her husband had achieved new levels of closeness and that she was at peace before dying.

It feels both odd and natural that I think to write to you on January 27: odd because you didn't actually know the Zantops; and natural because it's their murders thirteen years ago that brought you and me into contact twelve years ago. To be sure there's that "anniversary black cloud" hanging over me, but I'm doing okay because I had a really busy day of teaching, and I sure love my teaching. Also, I got to see Mom and Dad this weekend, and although things are sad at their house, there's also been a shift for the (ultimate) better, I believe.

I probably have to backtrack and let you know that Dad had a really bad Christmas. He seemed very depressed and since he was even more silent than usual, it was hard to guess what had changed for him internally. Factually speaking, he decided to stop trying to take even a few steps with his walker, so helping him use the toilet and transferring him from bed to wheelchair or armchair became essentially impossible for my mother to do. Most of us were home—the London crowd decided to remain in England for the second anniversary of Steve's death—so we had another family pow-wow on the topic of hospice. This time Mom agreed to it. Even writing that puts a little clench on my heart. It's been so hard for her to accept that Dad could die soon, and I get that; I really do.

While we made this decision and informed our local hospice of it just after Christmas, it took another three weeks for services to actually come into play—in other words, they just kicked in. The first nurse we were assigned took a medical leave, and the second doesn't seem all that interested in Dad's case. Still, we're grateful for the Hoyer lift that now makes it possible for anyone who learns how to use it (not difficult) to get Dad into or out of bed, onto or out of his chair. We haven't had much luck with aides either, but most weekdays someone comes for a few hours in the afternoon (and we're still paying our longtime helper for mornings and another helper for weekends). Mom manages to get out of the house a little bit, and for that we are very grateful. When I was home just now, Mom and I took an afternoon to look at the various cemetery options in their area, and while you could think that'd be depressing, taking the action felt positive to both of us, I believe. We certainly saw some beautiful spots. The public (rural) cemetery near our house which we loved exploring as kids is looking like the best option, and somehow that's comforting, too. I decided to buy the plot next to the one we're pretty sure Mom will buy for herself and Dad, and frankly, that feels like a load off my mind.

Which brings me to the other issue I really wanted to share with you: just one week ago at my church, we finally had a "green burial" seminar. I had attended one at another church last year (on my birthday, actually) and found it so helpful that I then began pushing to have one at our church; it finally came to fruition. Led by Lee Webster of New Hampshire Funeral Resources, Education, and Advocacy, the focus was on how to have a loved one's or your own funeral reflect your own values, not those of the funeral industry (a topic you and I have taken up before). What I found so compelling both last year and this was how making sure your funeral is ecologically friendly actually accords with ancient Christian burial practices (another topic we've discussed).

What Ms. Webster knows and explains particularly well are the discrepancies between what you're likely to be told by commercial funeral services and what the laws of your state actually are. To give you just one example, a concrete vault is required by some cemeteries, but it's not required by the State of Vermont or New Hampshire. Similarly, embalming may prolong slightly the onset of decay in the deceased, but in the meantime, it's poison to the embalmer as well as to the earth, and again, it's not required by law anywhere in our country. Lee Webster cited some statistics for the amount of embalming fluid, the amount of hardwoods, the amount of concrete that go into the earth each year in the United States as a result of our current mainstream funeral practices; they would make your head spin. Lest you think, as many do, that cremation is environmentally friendly, it turns out that it takes a huge amount of fossil fuel to generate enough heat to cremate a corpse and crush the bones.[4]

While, as with so many of the topics we've discussed, I would never want to dictate to other persons what they should want for themselves, I do want to spread the word about these issues. And, as I'd been thinking for a long time, I've made up my mind to go into the earth in as simple a container as the cemetery will accept, unembalmed and wearing a simple, cotton garb. One of the reasons that I got so excited about our local cemetery is that they don't require vaults. Hooray.

You and I have also discussed being with the corpse or a deceased loved one and what the benefit of that has been to each of us. Another extremely helpful element of the seminar was practicing washing, dressing, and moving the dead. Since I'd been at a similar event last year, I was the one who got to play the deceased. I was rather cavalier about it beforehand, but when I actually went to lie down on the massage table that was functioning as washing table to start playing my role, I panicked slightly and wondered if I should keep my eyes open or closed. I tried them out closed, then I opened them again: I found myself staring straight into the huge icon of Christ Pantocrator in the small dome of our church. I broke into a smile, and a few tears of joy rolled down my face before I closed my eyes again, realizing that everything was going to be okay. Better than okay. Perfect, really, now and in the future. I'm in God's hands—and hopefully will be in the hands of people I love, my co-parishioners who during the seminar were pretending to wash me and dress me. I stayed calm even as they practiced moving me and placing me in a, yes, real coffin. (One of our local Orthodox priests is a carpenter and makes beautiful but simple wooden coffins; we used one of his for the seminar. And then the person who had ordered it came to pick it up!) There it was in the making, Steve, that idea we'd talked about at our first Café mortel: a small team of friendly folk ready to go to the house of someone who's died and help with the preparation of the body. I do realize that if someone's coming at this topic "cold," what I'm reporting here could seem crazy. However, for me, anyway, being able to plan what I want for my own end has been one of the most concrete elements of having spent time mulling over human mortality with you.

    i.

Cornish, NH
May 15, 2014

Dear Irene,

When we started our exchanges almost three years ago, I had no idea where they would lead. Neither did you, I'm sure. I do know that, as we went along, we developed the hope that our conversation might be a model for other people who could have similar conversations with their own friends and families. I know that we both began with the belief that contemplating our mortality could make a difference not only in our deaths but also in our lives. And I know that we both still believe that.

I have been surprised, though, by where this conversation took us. So much of what I wrote, read, and thought was new to me. And while I don't think of myself as an expert on the end of life, I am around it enough that I had begun to feel myself comfortably set in my beliefs. Nothing chips away at that kind of comfort like having some of your beliefs challenged. I hope to continue the conversation, internally and with others, until I have just the perfect amount of experience with death to be an expert.

I met a woman a couple of years ago who had retired and moved out of the area. She was visiting a friend who had bought her a massage session. I have the uncommon tendency to get into conversations with my massage clients about dying and death, but this person was even more enthusiastic about the topic than I was. She told me that she had gotten to a point a year or two earlier when she wanted to talk about the end of life with her family—do a little planning, a little processing of her sense of being in the later stages of her life—but neither her husband nor her kids would engage with her. So instead, she and some friends who were having similar experiences created their own version of what you and I have been doing. Once a month, several woman ranging in age from their fifties to their eighties get together for a social gathering at which the topic of conversation can be anything under the umbrella of death and mortality. Embalming vs. cremation vs. whatever. No "heroic" life-lengthening measures vs. pull out all the stops. The spiritual and the practical. It's a Café mortel that was started by people who had never heard of a Café mortel.

I like the idea that their deaths might well be better for these gatherings, for having thought about how they would want them to unfold, what they would want to say or do beforehand, how they would want to be remembered. All of which would be a gift to themselves and to those loved ones too uncomfortable to have the conversations with them now.[5]

In the end, it is about letting go. Maybe not letting go entirely of the fear of death, but at least of the fear of talking about something as innately part of us as death. Letting go of the fear of living powerfully in the present, without the imagined comfort of the past and future. John O'Donohue wrote in his book *Anam Cara*: "When you begin to let go, it is amazing how enriched your life becomes. False things, which you have desperately held on to, move away very quickly from you. Then what is real, what you love deeply, and what really belongs to you comes deeper into you. No one can ever take them away from you."[6]

As I write this, I am taking a very deep breath, and trying, on the breathing out, to let go.

s.

White Plains, NY
30 June 2014

Dear Steve,

Dad died on June 20. My mother, one of my brothers, our long-term home health aide, and I were with him as he took his last breaths. This is the first opportunity I've had to sit down at my computer and try to write something. It strikes me that it is three years since I helped care for Dad while he was in the nursing home and also almost exactly three years since I started writing to you "formally" with my thoughts about mortality.

Thinking over the last weeks, I realize that, on the one hand, I was able to handle things so much more clearheadedly and peacefully because of all the "work"—all the topics I'd been able to think through on my own, with you, with Philippe, with my mother, with folks from my church. On the other hand, these experiences—actually living through Dad's last week of being alive and his dying moments by his side—have transformed me. To put it another way: I feel both like the self I've been for a while now, maybe since the aftermath of the Zantops' murders, and like someone a bit different because I've just been so close to death without dying myself. I'd mentioned to you before a few instances where I'd been with people I've loved shortly before they died or had sat with their corpses afterward. And now I've watched the moment of the transition itself. What a sacred mystery.

Dad had been breathing with great difficulty for a while, and some of his breathing in that last week did not sound so different to me from what I'd heard before. But from Sunday to Monday, even more strained and irregular breathing was accompanied by a horrible periodic spasm that would shake his whole body like a determined housewife shaking an area rug to get the dust out. It seemed to frighten him, and it was certainly keeping him awake. Early Monday morning, my mother and I telephoned a new friend of mine who's a palliative-care physician when we couldn't get our hospice on the line. On my friend's advice, we gave my father some extra anxiety medication. The woman who's been helping us with his care for almost three years arrived a bit later, washed him, and changed his clothes; she repositioned him in his bed, and he fell asleep. Hard to know which element helped him the most, but he slept peacefully for the next twenty-four hours! During that time, his regular doctor consulted with the hospice nurse, and they decided on a stronger pain medication that could be given to him in liquid form; all other medications were stopped except the anxiety med. You'll be happy to learn, I think, that during the day on Tuesday after he woke up from that long sleep, he had a professional massage from the masseuse I'd found last winter; that's the first time I was able to be present during a session. It was so obvious he was loving it, even though he couldn't say anything. One of the lightest moments we had that week came while she was massaging his scalp. He started moving his eyebrows in a way that made the masseuse and then us laugh. He appeared to be in a state of bliss, and our delighted reactions didn't rouse him from it.

Tuesday night, I discovered that he had vomited the applesauce he'd been fed just minutes earlier by the hospice aide, and that's when Mom and I realized his body could no longer process food. He essentially didn't drink from then on either. Mercifully and luckily, hospice was able to get us an experienced RN to stay with Dad through the night hours of Wednesday and Thursday. She knew how to make him comfortable in so many ways, like lubricating his lips with a small amount of olive oil and giving him just the right amount of pain meds just as he seemed to need them. On Friday morning, she said she thought it wouldn't be long now. Since she said she'd see us that night, I guess we still didn't think we were that close. But after she'd left, my mother and I sensed that something was different. I sat by his bed, just listening to that death-rattle breathing. I know you've heard that sound too and that most people find it uncomfortable to listen to. But knowing that it meant his end was near, I found myself able to tolerate it, looking into his face, stroking his beautiful silver hair, and sending loving thoughts. I canceled a doctor's appointment for my Mom that we were going to go to together; my Mom called our assigned hospice nurse and left her a message to please come as soon as she could; and I went to wake my brother, who'd just arrived from California a few hours prior. Our father still had a wonderful color in his face, and all parts of his body were warm, so again, we weren't sure we were that close, but our instincts kept telling us something was different. As his breathing became even more labored, we surrounded him: my mom on the side he was looking toward, my brother at the crown of his head, me on the other side of his head, and the aide at his feet. We told him how much we and all the family loved him. We had the sense he knew we were there.

The actual end came very quickly. All of a sudden—really within a second, I estimate—his face went from a natural-looking flush to a yellowish pallor. He breathed two more strained breaths, and his life was over.

So many thoughts come with trying to recount these events. I believe two are maybe the most direct fruits of the thinking I've been doing on mortality. First—and I notice I've already used the word *clearheaded*— my priorities felt so obvious: from the time it became clear to me that my father was dying, not falling to a new lower level of existence, I wanted to add to his comfort when possible and be as helpful to my mother as I could be. I wasn't tempted to replay old scenarios or second-guess decisions that I or others were making. I had originally been scheduled to be in Paris at a conference with my husband. At a certain point, it became crystal clear to me that Dad was dying, I wasn't leaving, and I didn't want to be anywhere else.

The second thought took me a bit by surprise in its palpability. The morning of his death, but before the actual last minutes, I had what felt like a luminous comprehension of the unity and brevity of life. My father was actually eighty-four-and-a-half years old at his death, and yet that seemed like such a short time to me during my epiphany: I felt like I could see him as a baby, kid, teenager, young adult, middle-aged parent, and an old man in practically an instant—in the same instant. I know they talk about your (own) life passing before your eyes in your dying moments. I have no idea if that was happening for my father; to be honest, he actually seemed pretty anchored in the present. In any case, I connected this insight, too, with priorities: so little of what we normally fuss about can have meaning in the face of how short life really is. Is that one meaning of the John O'Donohue lines you quoted to me about letting go? "False things, which you have desperately held on to, move away very quickly from you. Then what is real, what you love deeply, and what really belongs to you comes deeper into you. No one can ever take them away from you."

So here are some other fruits of having thought so much about end of life and about how I hoped it would go for him: After my father died, the hospice nurse who had gotten our message and come over pronounced him dead, we called our siblings, our father's sister, and the priest; the priest came and said a prayer. Then we took care of his body, something I have written about to you as an ancient Christian practice that is also being revived in more and more Jewish American communities, and that some parts of the green-burial movement emphasize, too. We gently washed him, we anointed him, we dressed him, and we re-laid him on his bed on clean sheets, brought the icon of his patron saint and of the Virgin and child (tradition would have it be an icon of the Resurrection, but we didn't have one), put ice under him and kept him with us in the house. My mother's sister from Florida just happened to be visiting with her son and another niece, and the three of them drove over from New Jersey to be with us and pay respects to Dad. Their presence was very special, too. That evening folks from the funeral home came to pick up my father's relic, as we refer in our tradition to the body when the soul has left it. Each step felt perfectly natural, perfectly like what we wanted to be doing. In fact, anything else would have been weird.

And that's how all the rest of it has gone for me, Steve: the final plans with the funeral home, the wake, the funeral, the burial, the funeral meal, the first steps of setting his affairs in order. It's all been just fine. We are sad sometimes, of course, especially when our mother is feeling sad—her daily pattern of life for nine plus years has been completely dissolved. And she's lost her life partner of sixty years. Talk about change! As for me, I feel calm and above all very, very grateful. I couldn't prevent or alter anything, really, in the course of his disease, but I do have a sense that I contributed to decisions about how he would be cared for that added to his comfort and were in line with what he wanted for himself. I feel incredibly grateful that I was by his side so much in these last years. Especially during his last days, I was feeling as pure a compassion as I imagine we flawed mortals can feel. As Steve Levine suggests in his book *Who Dies?* when nothing else can be done, just send love.[7] With every fiber of my being, I sat by my father's side and sent love.

I feel humbled by everything that led me to be able to do these things: all the reading, all the discussing, all the trying out of various scenarios in my head and with my mother; all the actual planning, like scouting cemeteries, purchasing a plot, speaking with a funeral director, looking at caskets. I realize now that each of those little actions helped me wrap my mind more concretely around the reality of his actual death that was likely coming soon and that now has come.

People mean well and blurt out: I'm so sorry. I smile and say thank you. But each time I've heard those words, I think to myself: I'm not sorry. I'm not sorry he got to die at home. I'm not sorry hospice stepped up to the plate when it really mattered. I'm not sorry he got proper pain and anxiety medication. I'm not sorry he was surrounded by family as he died. I'm not sorry he was prayed over as his soul separated from his body. I'm not sorry his body was gently washed, anointed, and then dressed by people who knew and loved him. Here's a vision that will comfort me for a long time to come: my younger brother giving our father his last shave. Pete did that so lovingly and so expertly; as he did it, he recounted our father teaching him to shave. There's an alternate image of the life cycle. Finally, I'm not sorry that my father gave me the huge gift of going to his death before me and showing me that it can be done and that I don't need to be afraid of this great gift of mortality.

Be well, dear friend. Thank you for going this long and often-uncomfortable way with me.

Peace! I feel like I can finally claim it as my name,

Irene

Cornish, NH
August 4, 2014

Good morning, Irene,

You noted it yourself a while back: It was your Dad who you thought would be the first to die of the three family members nearing their ends when we started writing to each other. That he was the last to die says nothing in particular, except that there is no knowing.

I won't say I'm sorry, except for the grief I know you are experiencing for the loss of your father. After all of the ups and downs you and your family have seen during his last few years, it seems as though it could not have gone better in the end. Just a beautiful story. On its own, it is reason enough for anyone who hears or reads it to begin to think deeply about life, death, and mortality.

You describe the experience as a beginning arising from an ending. Something new coming from something passing. That's true for him if there really is an eternal life after death. And it's true for you, from what you say about how his death has changed you. You're different now. A small rebirth. We can all hope for the same.

It might seem a stretch, but I'm going to use this as a segue into another story. And really, I don't need much of a segue to tell a story, as you've found out. This one is about a beginning and an ending, too. And since it involves one of my granddaughters, I can't resist telling it.

About 120 miles separate Portsmouth, New Hampshire, from Thetford, Vermont. About 120 miles and, on one day in May 2009, a lifetime. My first grandchild was born on May 19 of that year, a beautiful girl who arrived to the name Molly Jean Elizabeth. My wife and I were with her and her parents in Portsmouth shortly after her birth, and as other grandparents know, there is nothing like that first sight, first touch, first nose-to-nose. She slept all but a few minutes of the several hours I was there, and with her eyes closed, her breath gentle and even, she seemed perfectly angelic. I stared at her a lot, wondering what was happening behind those smooth eyelids, wondering what lay in her future. So much, and all of it a mystery.

Later in the day, I left to return to work. My wife was staying on for a couple of days, so I said good-bye to my expanded family and headed for Thetford to see a Hand to Heart client. It was another in a series of visits with a fifty-eight-year-old woman who was nearing her death. I had been visiting Diane with my massage table for several weeks, since she had returned home from the hospital with the expectation that she might live only a week or two. But she'd hung around, aware that she would die soon, mostly at peace with that, and apparently in no hurry.

For the first weeks, she could get onto the massage table with assistance, and the massages seemed to help, easing some of the physical discomfort and smoothing some of the emotional rough edges. By the second week of May, she could no longer get on the table, and received her massages while lying on a daybed in the middle of her small home. Each time I saw her, she was less alert, further into her journey away from this life. We had come to know a lot about each other, and she would occasionally ask if my grandchild had arrived yet. Just several days before Molly's arrival, Diane roused herself from sleep to ask about it again. When I said no, she gestured impatiently, if weakly, with her hand and said with a bit of a smile, "That baby *has* to be born."

And then she was. When I arrived at Diane's house on May 19, her partner and caregiver met me outside and told me that she'd been asleep most of the last twenty-four hours, that she hadn't moved much at all, and that she seemed comfortable. I went in on my own and sat next to the daybed. Placing my hand lightly on her belly, I said quietly, "Hi, Diane."

Her eyes opened halfway. She saw me and smiled, moving a hand toward me. I took her hand and said: "Guess who got to hold his brand-new baby granddaughter today."

Her eyes shot open like saucers. "*Really*?" she asked.

"Really," I said.

Immediately she started fading and dropping back to her pillow, but as she did, she kept repeating, "That's good. That's good. A baby. That's good." In half a minute, she was asleep again. I did some gentle massage, during which she stirred only a little. I looked into her face, studying it closely, and wondered what was happening behind it and what was ahead for her.

Outside, I told her partner about the exchange. He told me that Diane had always been intensely committed to the idea that girls should grow up with the same opportunities and possibilities as boys, so he wasn't surprised that she'd connected so strongly with the birth of a new little girl, especially as she was leaving.

I saw Diane once more, two days later. She didn't wake up when I arrived and put my hands on her, but shortly before I left, I leaned over, kissed her on the forehead, and said, "Travel safely, Diane." She opened her eyes a bit and whispered, "You're leaving?"

"Shortly," I said.

"Where are you going?"

"Well, I'm going off to work. But right now, I'm just sitting here with you." She smiled slightly.

After a moment, I asked: "Where are *you* going?"

"I'm going somewhere today," she answered with another weak smile. Then she slept.

As it turned out, she was off by about half a day; Diane died the following morning.

When I told her partner that I had been watching her and wondering what she was thinking and what was next for her, he said, "I can tell you that Diane thinks she is going on an amazing adventure."

Just like Molly.

Keep in touch, even if only occasionally.

Steve

Lebanon, NH

5 February 2015

Dear Steve,

I think way back when, I told you about a book by a psychiatrist who himself struggled with brain cancer, wrote about it, and died. All of a sudden, the title of his last book makes a lot more sense to me: *On peut se dire au revoir plusieurs fois* (literally: "One can say good-bye numerous times").[8] I feel like we keep saying good-bye to each other, at least in our correspondence, and then one of us feels the need to write again. I suppose this is just fine and dandy as long as the other of us is willing to read and respond. Here's another observation about us writing to each other for so long: we stay in touch over years, and one of us could find out he or she is ill, seriously ill, or maybe not so seriously ill. Hard to know which at this point.

Yesterday I got a phone call that I imagine every adult woman is both expecting and at the same time hoping to never get. "We received your biopsy results. You have breast cancer," I heard the doctor say . . .

REAPING THE BENEFITS
OF OUR EXCHANGE

Cornish, NH
February 17, 2015

Dear Irene,

I can think of quite a few times in our writing and our conversations when you said, in reference to whatever aspect of dying or mortality we were discussing, something along the lines of "This could happen to either one of us at any time, God forbid." I remember you using almost those exact words once when we were sitting at your dining-room table, going over a section of this book. It was very hard to be sitting at that same table this morning and hear you tell me more about your cancer diagnosis.

I am so sorry. Whenever I considered what you said about such a thing happening to either one of us, I think I processed it as happening to me. It's hard to think of you now having to deal with such news, and with the treatments and uncertainties that will follow. I can almost imagine it as you starting this book all over from the beginning, only for real. Is your cancer unfair or unjust? Will you be open to the care that those who love you will want to provide? What kind of pain might you experience and what choices will you make for dealing with it? Can you be in the moment for each moment?

That last seems like the toughest part, at least to me. And of course, it's very early, too early to know what exactly the challenges will be. But I don't know anyone who is as deeply thoughtful as you, so I know you will face it with a clear head and an open heart.

I won't presume to give you any advice, but I will offer this observation: It's not a linear process. There isn't a start point and an end point and a straight line between them. There are ups and downs, good days followed by bad days, and vice versa. I think that is often what people feel is the hardest part to deal with. Your faith, your family, and your many friends—they will all be your certainty when there doesn't seem to be any.

Please let me know how you're doing, and how I can help.

Steve

Lebanon, NH
18 February 2015

Dear Steve,

Thanks for coming over and thanks for writing. (Funny how natural writing to each other feels in this day of cell phones, texting, and social media.) I appreciated that you wanted to reach out when you got my news, and I was comforted by seeing you and hearing your voice, even as I didn't want to talk for long. I hope you can understand. It's not that I'm refusing to acknowledge my diagnosis. Rather, it is all pretty confusing right now. I feel the profound need to get my thoughts in order for myself before I interact much with other people. Given me and my habits, it won't surprise you that I've hardly told anyone, not even my family. Well, of course my husband knows. Other than hashing it out with him, I've been trying to clarify things for myself by writing. I've started a "cancer diary," and it's helping me register my feelings about being in this situation. I am aware that there is so much writing on breast cancer out there, especially in the form of memoirs and blogs, even as I'm completely uninterested in reading any of them right now and uninterested in sharing most of my own thoughts with anyone else. I know that you have had many clients with cancer, including breast cancer, so there's lots I don't need to rehearse with you here.

There was a several-day-long "black hole" in my medical care between THE PHONE CALL and my request to my health clinic for guidance on what to do next. I felt like I'd been disconnected from any doctor I'd had contact with. Even my primary-care physician was out sick. Ironically, in relation to that vacuum, I then quickly found myself placed onto the gigantic medico-technological breast-cancer-treatment conveyor belt that is the Norris Cotton Cancer Center: MRI scheduled for Monday; appointment with the surgeon on Wednesday; a book and a DVD with my options to be studied before the Wednesday appointment; an MRI biopsy to check several additional suspicious spots; genetic testing; and so on. Just promised you I wouldn't rehearse it, and here I am listing things. Hmmmmm.

What's most on my mind that I set out to share with you is that I do not want to become my diagnosis. I believe I'm being genuinely honest with myself and now with you that I am not afraid to die. I'm not afraid to die as much as I am afraid that whatever life I have in front of me will become "just" the hospital, just the tests, just the treatments, just the recoveries. I shared with you long ago my discomfort with the rhetoric of "battling cancer"; I realize now that in addition to my general aversion to any metaphors of war, such frameworks define the participant only in terms of the disease. I've been told hardly anything about this cancer because they don't know much yet. But I guess I'm feeling right now that the scenario I put myself through years ago still holds: If there's something obvious to test or treat, I want to do it. But if treatment starts to take over my life, I will stop it.

Here's a related thought: One of the things that was very confusing for me about my father's and my mother-in-law's decline was a perception that they were loving the attention that came to them as a result of their physical problems. As self-focused as I have felt lately (from the "additional views" through the biopsy and the wait for the biopsy results and now walking through the system for breast-cancer victims—yick, I hate that phrase), I don't think it's that kind of attention I crave. So, again, it's not the dying that preoccupies me right now, it's the "how do I live when I know I'm going to die." There's actually a book by that title.[1] It's not a very helpful book—at least it wasn't for me—but the title sure does capture what's on my mind.

So here's something else I put in my cancer diary: Whether I am close or far in terms of my mortal end—and we've said a couple of times that in the scheme of things, whether you die in childhood, middle age, or so-called old age, all human life is short—I want to become even more the person I've been striving to be this half century of my conscious life. There's the living in the present that I've talked about before. Right now that would mean not ignoring my moments of panic, despair, or denial. These have been brief; still, I've tried not to pretend that I was not feeling what I was feeling. (There's meaning to be mined from those grammatical negatives, I suspect.) At the same time, I've tried to hear my instantaneous evaluation of myself as completely childish when I protest receiving a cancer diagnosis, even if I'm only protesting to myself. Living in the present right now also means not obsessing in advance over what tests will reveal or what treatments will be recommended. Similarly, it means registering the joy of eating dinner with my husband or of teaching my classes. It also means being nice to the people behind those voices who are scheduling my appointments (especially if I've been on hold for a long time) or with whomever else I'm coming in contact in other situations related to my diagnosis. I fear this sounds cloying. Yet I'm powerfully reminded of one lesson I learned in the wake of the Zantops' murders: If this is my last moment (granted, moment defined generously here: not even in my most pessimistic mood do I think I'm going to die soon—not from cancer anyway), I want to spend it as happily as possible. I want the persons I've interacted with, even if it's "merely" an exchange of glances, to feel good about what just happened, not angry, annoyed, or depressed. So, yes, I tell myself, go ahead and let it out: I DON'T WANT TO HAVE CANCER, but don't wallow in that thought.

That I've got to be vigilant about behaving in ways that reflect the person I consider myself to be came through a scene yesterday. The teacher of the class before mine ran over his allotted class time, and when he tried to apologize, I gruffly snapped that he was late and this wasn't the first time. That felt awful even as the words were coming out of my mouth. And I realized pretty quickly that the unwarranted meanness had nothing to do with him and everything to do with my recent news and not sleeping well.

To get back to another set of reflections we've shared: no, I don't think God gave me this cancer. But I do think that finding myself here, I can search for the good, for the many good things that might be coming my way, that I might contribute to making happen, as a result of it.

I won't claim to have achieved it just yet, but my goal is to spend as much time feeling gratitude as possible. I wrote you long ago: I have lived such a rich life, a life that's had deep joys and profound losses. Both are good. You can't feel profound loss if you haven't loved deeply. Bringing gratitude to the here and now: what a blessing—call it good luck if you prefer—that there was an MRI appointment available so quickly; what a blessing that the head breast-cancer surgeon had a cancelation for a few days later; what a blessing that the second MRI did not reveal additional tumors; what a blessing that all the folks I have had to speak with on the phone, including the doctor who first gave me the news, were so very gentle and competent. (She even gave me her private cell-phone number and said not to hesitate to call if I wanted to at any point later that day or in the near future.) What a gift to have registered all that *as it was happening* and to say to the people involved: thank you.

Here's something I want to add to Stephen Levine's "when there's nothing left to do, just send love." No matter what's going on, don't forget to register the good, to be thankful for it, and to express those thanks: to the other mortals involved, to the Supreme Being if you believe in one.

Whatever's headed my way, dear friend, I think I'm going to be okay. I know that neither of us saw this coming, but what a great preparation you've helped me have to be in this place. And let's not forget to laugh that here we are trying to finish a book on mortality and one of us gets a cancer diagnosis! Didn't you have a client who told her husband she was going to deal with cancer her way, and that meant with laughter?

To get back to that battling-cancer metaphor, I think I've got my replacement: I'm in training—training to be as healthy and positive as I can be for each step of this unexpected journey. I don't plan to battle anyone or anything. I do plan to take care of myself, as I also plan to be careful with all the people in relationships I have now or will develop. I know that my earthly journey's end is death of the body, whenever that end arrives. I've made my death plan and communicated it in writing and orally to all the people who are likely to be involved. I'm ready and I'm not afraid. Just endlessly grateful—and a little anxious now and then.

RESOURCES AND INSPIRATIONS FOR CONTINUED THINKING ABOUT MORTALITY

W e offer below some suggestions to help readers continue to develop their thinking on mortality. In appendix A, we've grouped those suggestions around what might be your own current position. So, the first section continues the vein of "ordinary mortals," that is, those who are not necessarily ill or taking care of an ill loved one, but rather who, like Irene and Steve at the beginning of the journey followed in this book, simply feel the need to think about how the fact that our lives will end might change how we are living our lives right now. The second section addresses caregivers. The third is for folks who learn or have known for a while that they have a disease that will probably lead to their mortal end, and for their loved ones. Appendix B is designed for those who are in reading groups or would like to start one to think about these subjects together. Here we also list some great literature to read alone or with a group.

Of course, many of the resources we've mentioned in the main part of this book or are mentioning here in the appendices are relevant to more than one of the categories we've set up. And our readers will notice that some situations have been more thoroughly addressed to date than others. Our hope is that perhaps one day soon books or other materials will be written offering guidance in those areas. We, obviously, cannot be exhaustive in our offerings of additional resources.

Finally, these lists have not been vetted by some committee of death experts as the "go-to" sources on these subjects; rather, they merely represent what we have run across and found most helpful in our attempts to come to terms with life's biggest mystery.

APPENDIX A

Suggested Resources and Inspirations for Ordinary Mortals

Barthes, Roland. *Journal de deuil. 26 octobre 1977–15 septembre 1979*. Text established and annotated by Nathalie Léger. Paris: Seuil/Imec, 2009.

———. *Mourning Diary*. Translated by and with an afterword by Richard Howard. New York: Hill and Wang, 2012. Moving reflections written on scraps of paper by the great French intellectual Roland Barthes in the wake of his mother's death.

Beauvoir, Simone de. *Une Mort très douce*. Paris: Gallimard, 1964.

———. *A Very Easy Death*. Translated by Patrick O'Brian. New York: Pantheon, 1965. Though published fifty years ago, Simone de Beauvoir's account of her mother's painful death offers much to ponder, particularly about family relations in the context of terminal illness and about the dangers lurking in "treatment."

Ben Jalloun, Tahar. *Sur ma mère*. (About My Mother.) Paris: Gallimard, 2008. A moving, lyrical account by a major novelist and French intellectual of his illiterate mother's life and death. Currently available only in French.

Bloom, Harold, ed. *Till I End My Song: A Gathering of Last Poems*. New York: Harper, 2010. This is a noteworthy collection of poems that were the last or nearly the last written by a wide range of poets, from the little-known to the famous. Plenty to think about here.

Brown, Erica. *Happier Endings: A Meditation on Life and Death*. New

York: Simon & Schuster, 2013. In a wonderfully readable combination of scholarship and story, Brown does in her own way what we set out to do when we began to work on this book: change the experience of both life and death. She does it well. Among the many gems to be found in her book: "We have created, very possibly, the worst of all possible worlds when it comes to death and aging: we have the capacity to keep people alive longer than they can maintain a desirable quality of life." And, "The forgiveness habit is both lifelong, and has long-life dividends."

Byock, Ira. *The Best Care Possible: A Physician's Quest to Transform Care through the End of Life*. New York: Avery (Penguin), 2012. Byock is one of the leading figures in transforming palliative care in this country. This is one of several books he's written on the topic of caring for those at end of life, especially in institutions.

Cave, Stephen. *Immortality: The Quest to Live Forever and How It Drives Civilization*. New York: Crown, Random House, 2012. If you want to think about where your own feelings about life, death, and mortality fit into the big picture of human history, this book is a good place to start.

Cohen, Lewis M. *No Good Deed: A Story of Medicine, Murder Accusations, and the Debate over How We Die*. 2010; repr., New York: Harper, 2011. A chilling account written by an MD of an incident in Massachusetts in which two nurses were accused of killing a patient because they had given her morphine to ease her pain at end of life. Cohen uses this specific occurrence to explore the legal and ethical dilemmas of modern medicine.

Crettaz, Bernard. *vous parler de la mort*. Ayer: Editions Porte-plumes, 2003. This little book offers wide-ranging thoughts on human mortality from the individual who dedicated his whole career to helping people think about death. Currently available only in French.

Dialogues des Carmélites de F. Poulenc. (Dialogues of the Carmelites of F. Poulenc.) Directed by Marthe Keller and Don Kent. Bel Air classiques, 2011. DVD. This opera revolves around individuals who are faced with violent death because of persecution of the religious by French Revolutionaries. Poulenc was a committed Roman Catholic and projects himself into these historical figures with particular compassion.

Kacandes, Irene. "1/27/01=9/11/01: The Changed Posttraumatic Self." In *Trauma at Home: After 9/11*, edited by Judith Greenberg, pp. 168–83. Lincoln: University of Nebraska Press, 2003. This essay details Irene's experience of the sudden and violent deaths of her friends Susanne Zantop and Half Zantop and offers one illustration of trying to carry on after traumatic loss.

Kübler-Ross, Elisabeth. *Living with Death and Dying*. New York: Simon & Schuster, 1997. Born in Switzerland, psychiatrist Kübler-Ross lived most of her adult life in the United States. Eventually authoring dozens of books, *On Death and Dying* (originally published in 1969) outlined her theory of the five stages of grief, which, though disputed for its rigidity, is still the basis for much thinking and advice on grieving. The book recommended here takes up grief and much more, offering narratives of families in the throes of difficult decisions about treatment and living with the consequences of those decisions.

Lynch, Thomas. *Bodies in Motion and at Rest: On Metaphor and Mortality*. New York: W. W. Norton, 2001. Lynch is both a poet and a funeral director. The unusual combination makes for a collection of fascinating essays about America's relationship with death and the dead.

Montross, Christine. *Body of Work: Meditations on Mortality from the Human Anatomy Lab*. New York: Penguin, 2007. A beautifully written hybrid text: part remembrances of her first class in medical school, part historical investigation into the history of dissection, part elegy for beloved family members. Poet/psychiatrist Montross offers readers much to think about.

Noys, Benjamin. *The Culture of Death*. Oxford and New York: Berg, 2005.

This book is for the most theoretically and philosophically minded of our readers. It offers perspectives on postmodern society's views of death, particularly in light of the downgrading of the value of individual life set in motion by the twin catastrophes of genocide and totalitarianism of the mid-twentieth century.

Nuland, Sherwin B. *How We Die, Reflections on Life's Final Chapter*. New York: Vintage Books, 1993. Nuland takes his readers through the details of what happens to the body and mind as people die of illness (such as heart disease and cancer), violence, old age, dementia, and more.

Oppliger, Simone. *L'Amour mortel*. (Fatal Love.) Orbe: Bernard Campiche Editeur, 2010. Originally published in 1986. Photographer Simone Oppliger narrates the story of and ruminates on the violent death of her dear friend G. Beautifully written. Currently available only in French.

Roach, Mary. *Stiff: The Curious Lives of Human Cadavers*. New York: W. W. Norton, 2003. Roach is the author of a number of lighthearted books on topics ranging from sex to the alimentary canal. This one considers the often-bizarre relationship we have with human remains, which, after all, must say something about our relationship with death.

Schmemann, Alexander. *O Death, Where Is Thy Sting?* Yonkers, New York: St. Vladimir's Seminary, 2003. Another book for the more philosophically minded, as Orthodox theologian Schmemann addresses the origins of death.

Suggested Resources and Inspirations for Caregivers

Amour. Directed by Michael Haneke. Sony Pictures Home Entertainment, 2013. DVD. Winner of a 2012 Academy Award, Haneke's film offers a particularly poignant, because unsentimental and sustained, look at caregiving by family members.

Callanan, Maggie, and Patricia Kelley. *Final Gifts*. New York, Bantam

Books, 1992. Written by a couple of hospice nurses, this book offers stories and insights about how to be with and listen to people who are dying. Years later, Callanan came out with a follow-up collection of stories and lessons called *Final Journeys* (New York: Bantam Dell, 2008).

Halifax, Joan. *Being with Dying: Cultivating Compassion and Fearlessness in the Presence of Death*. Boston: Shambala Publications, 2008.

———. *Being with Dying*. Sounds True Inc., 1997. Audiobook CD. Joan Halifax can be listened to or read with great profit by anyone, but her vocation involves reorienting, enhancing, and supporting the efforts of all kinds of caregivers to the dying. Halifax began her life as a Christian and became a Buddhist. This work is imbued with her Buddhist orientation to dying and death.

Halt auf freier Strecke. (Stopped on Track.) Directed by Andreas Dresen. Peter Rommel Productions, 2011. DVD. About a young father who receives a diagnosis of inoperable brain cancer. Director Dresen used many professional caregivers (that is, nonactors) in the movie and achieved a marvelously unsentimental examination of the trials of tending to the terminally ill.

Levine, Stephen, and Ondrea Levine. *Who Dies? An Investigation of Conscious Living and Conscious Dying*. New York; Toronto: Anchor Books, 1989. This book can be read with regard to almost any aspect of mortality. However, Irene and Steve have been particularly inspired by its descriptions of caregivers going about their work of accompanying the dying. Levine shares, for instance, his work with dying children. Many other caretakers' actions are included in the book. It has a strong Buddhist orientation but shows openness to spirituality of any stripe.

Macmillan Cancer Support. "In the Last Few Weeks." http://www.macmillan.org.uk/Cancerinformation/Endoflife/Thelastfewweeks.aspx. Accessed July 22, 2015. This particular webpage from the Macmillan Cancer Support website offers a concrete description of the last few weeks of life. Macmillan Cancer Support is a registered charity in the United Kingdom, and its website offers a wealth of information in clear language.

Today's Caregiver. www.caregiver.com. Accessed July 22, 2015. Today's Caregiver is a commercial site that also sponsors a free newsletter you can have delivered to your e-mail inbox (from newsletters@caregiver.com). The topics taken up there are very specifically addressed to caregivers, and individuals can also write in with a specific concern and receive responses from other individuals who have dealt with similar problems. The site and newsletter point to many other resources, not all of equal value in our view, but many of which are sound and helpful. You can also write to the organization at a street address: Today's Caregiver, 3350 Griffin Road, Fort Lauderdale, FL 33312.

Suggested Resources and Inspirations for Individuals with Life-Changing Illness and Their Families

Barna, J. Mark, and Elizabeth J. Barna. *A Christian Ending: A Handbook for Burial in the Ancient Christian Tradition*. Manton, CA: Divine Ascent, 2011. For years, the two laypeople who authored this book have been taking care of fellow parishioners who have died; they finally decided to share their methods with the larger public. The first part of the book outlines their own understanding of ancient Christian practices of burial, modeled on how Christ's body was treated by his disciples, and the second offers a hands-on explanation of how others could go about turning themselves into small groups ready to help prepare the deceased for burial. There is also a series of appendices with forms that can be used to express one's wishes for end of life. Strong Christian orientation.

Butler, Katy. *Knocking on Heaven's Door: The Path to a Better Way of Death*. New York: Scribner, 2013. Though exquisitely painful to read, Butler's wrenching account of her father's illness and death is very helpful for families trying to find their way through the medical system. With carefully researched information about healthcare and particularly about pacemakers, the book offers readers the chance to think through what they would want to do if they find themselves facing similar choices to those that Butler's family faced.

Gawande, Atul. *Being Mortal: Medicine and What Matters in the End.* New York: Metropolitan Books, 2014. An unflinching look at our current system for end-of-life care, with some background on how we got here and some strong advice for patients and families about maintaining personal priorities when selecting medical treatment. Currently on many bestseller lists, and rightly so, in our view.

Hennezel, Marie de. *Intimate Death: How the Dying Teach Us How to Live.* Translated from French by Carol Janeway. New York: Vintage, 1998. A psychologist in a French hospital, Marie de Hennezel has worked with AIDS patients for many years. Here she speaks of lessons on life she believes she has learned from all her patients. De Hennezel is a prolific author on mortality; many of her other books have also been translated into English.

Hoppe, Lynette Katherine, and Father Luke Alexander Veronis. *Lynette's Hope: The Witness of Lynette Katherine Hoppe's Life and Death.* Ben Lomond, CA: Conciliar Press Ministries, 2008. This book offers excerpts from the diary of a young woman missionary to Albania who learned she had advanced breast cancer, and it also offers the testimony of those who accompanied Lynette on the final legs of her earthly journey. It illustrates the strong belief of an Eastern Orthodox Christian that mortal death is not the end.

Huisman-Perrin, Emmanuelle. *La Mort expliquée à ma fille.* (Death Explained to My Daughter.) Paris: Seuil, 2002. This short book models for parents how they might choose to respond to their children's questions about death. Currently available only in French.

Karnes, Barbara. *The Final Act of Living: Reflections of a Longtime Hospice Nurse.* Vancouver, WA: Barbara Karnes Books, 2003. Revised 2012.

Writing in clear, direct language, Karnes synthesizes for readers her experience and lessons learned. In many regards, this is the gentlest and yet most helpful introduction to human mortality Irene and Steve have run across. If you are being forced to think about these issues for the first time, consider starting with Karnes.

Kessler, David. *The Needs of the Dying: A Guide for Bringing Hope, Comfort and Love to Life's Final Chapter*. New York: Harper, 2007. This is the tenth anniversary edition of Kessler's book (originally released in hardcover with the title *The Rights of the Dying*). In it, he offers lessons and stories on a range of topics that will benefit both the dying person and those caring for him or her. Kessler was a collaborator of Elisabeth Kübler-Ross.

Kübler-Ross, Elisabeth. *On Children and Death: How Children and Their Parents Can and Do Cope with Death*. New York: Simon & Schuster, 1997. The title may say it all. Kübler-Ross offers guidance on how to cope with this excruciatingly sad experience that was, of course, much more common in earlier periods than our own.

Lynn, Joanne, Joan K. Harrold, and Janice Lynch Schuster. *Handbook for Mortals: Guidance for People Facing Serious Illness*. 2nd ed. New York; Oxford: Oxford University Press, 2011. First published in 1999 by two physicians and updated and republished with a third author in 2011, this handbook offers excellent information on subjects important to and yet often not well understood by patients (for instance, about pain medication or bodily changes as the result of illness). Irene and Steve recommend it particularly for its suggestions and checklists that patients and their families can use when speaking with physicians and other professional caregivers.

Schwalbe, Will. *The End of Your Life Book Club*. London: Two Roads Books, 2012. A memoir of Schwalbe's accompaniment of his active and witty mother at her end of life. The title concerns the series of books the two decided to read and then discuss during the mother's chemotherapy infusions.

Servan-Schreiber, David, with Ursula Gauthier. *Not the Last Good-bye: On Life, Death, Healing, and Cancer*. Translation copyright held by Susanna Lea Associates. New York: Viking Penguin, 2011. (Original: *On peut se dire au revoir plusieurs fois*. Paris: Éditions Robert Laffont, 2011.) A successful psychiatrist at University of Pittsburgh School of Medicine, Servan-Schreiber was diagnosed with brain cancer at age thirty and reoriented his endeavors to fighting cancer through healthy living. His books *The Instinct to Heal* (2004) and *Anticancer* (2008) became international bestsellers. In *Not the Last Good-bye*, a small and moving book, Servan-Schreiber describes the return of his own cancer and shares his thoughts as his faces his imminent death in his native France. He died on July 24, 2011.

APPENDIX B

Suggested Resources and Inspirations for Group Discussion

The books and other resources mentioned in any of the above lists could be read and discussed with profit by a group. In fact, any book, fiction or nonfiction, that deals with important questions about life and death, and life *with* death, could be a good starting point for a group discussion.

Irene and Steve mention in several chapters of *Let's Talk about Death* the Cafés mortels originally organized by Swiss sociologist Bernard Crettaz. These were social gatherings taking place in commercial cafés or pubs, planned for the purpose of allowing people to discuss issues related to the end of life, gatherings at which the stigma or reluctance that usually accompany that topic were dropped. Irene and Steve organized a few such meetings themselves, inviting friends and colleagues to join them for snacks and conversation in Irene's home. A diverse group of people arrived for the first meeting, each with his or her experiences and curiosities about death and dying. Most were individuals in good health at the time, although one woman had incurable colon cancer. Her openness and generosity of spirit made everyone else in the group comfortable in her presence, and the discussion was lively, moving from topic to topic. If there was a dominant theme, it might have been that people recall the illnesses and deaths of people close to them as examples of how they might want to, or might *not* want to, face their own deaths. There's no trick to organizing your own Café mortel—or whatever you might call it. Invite friends, neighbors, coworkers, and family. Make the atmosphere as relaxed and inviting as possible through comfortable seating, good light, and perhaps snacks and beverages. Whoever shows up is at least starting with the curiosity needed to be part of the discussion.

Below we list some books we think lend themselves particularly well to group discussion.

Chast, Roz. *Can't We Talk about Something More Pleasant? A Memoir.* New York: Bloomsbury, 2014. A hilarious and painful memoir of the *New Yorker* cartoonist Roz Chast's attempts to care for her two aging parents when they themselves did not want to do any planning for end of life. The visual and the verbal texts interact in interesting ways that make for great discussion material. It's such a relief to be able to laugh at some of this. You're likely to flinch and cry, too.

Crettaz, Bernard. *Cafés mortels: Sortir la mort du silence.* (Death Cafés: Bring Death out of the Silence.) Geneva: Editions Labor et Fides, 2010. This short book offers a history of the Cafés mortels from the originator of the idea, Swiss sociologist Bernard Crettaz. He describes the settings he chose in ordinary cafés, the variety of people who have showed up to participate, and the topics that typically have come up, with his responses to them. You might bristle a bit at his own presumptions of authority on the topic, but then again, he did spend his whole adult life thinking about death.

Gutkind, Lee, ed. *At the End of Life: True Stories about How We Die.* 2011; repr., Pittsburgh: Creative Nonfiction Books, 2012. These short stories, essays, and accounts written by doctors, nurses, and family members do not shrink from portraying the negative side of the medicalization of death. Their genuineness and intensity are very moving and sure to help launch discussion. Many of the pieces are short and could even be read aloud during a group discussion.

Schels, Walter, and Beate Lakotta. *Noch Mal Leben vor dem Tod: Wenn Menschen Sterben.* (To Live Again before Dying: When People Die.) Munich: Deutsche Verlags-Anstalt, 2004. Though this book is currently available only in German, Irene suggests that its gorgeous and affecting photographs could be looked at by your group and discussed. What signs do we use to distinguish the paired photographs, that is, that in one photo the person is alive and in the other that same person dead?

Vitello, Paul. "Reviving a Ritual of Tending to the Dead," *New York Times*, December 12, 2010, http://www.nytimes.com/2010/12/13/nyregion/13burial.html?pagewanted=all&_r=0. For those groups that might want to take their activities beyond reading and discussion, we can recommend learning more about lay groups educating themselves on attending to the dead. This article describes Jewish laypeople choosing to learn about traditional Jewish customs for preparing the dead for burial. See also the Barna book on ancient Christian burial mentioned in appendix A.

Wallace, David Foster. *This Is Water: Some Thoughts, Delivered on a Significant Occasion, about Living a Compassionate Life.* New York: Little, Brown, 2009. This book could make an excellent choice for actually reading aloud with your group, laughing together, pausing over illustrative scenarios together, pondering how each member might choose to practice her or his own version of "living a compassionate life."

Suggested Works of Literature Dealing with Mortality

Especially for a literature professor like Irene, it seems folly to suggest a short list of works of literature that deal with mortality, since it would not be inaccurate to say that death is the theme par excellence of great literature. However, in the spirit of sharing what particularly came to our minds as we were taking this journey of thinking about mortality, we offer the following titles, even as we are not foolish enough to try to annotate them. Any of them could make a great focus for a group discussion.

Broch, Hermann. *The Death of Virgil*. Translated by Jean Starr Untermeyer. New York: Vintage, 1995. German original published in 1945.

Delibes, Miguel. *Cinco horas con Mario*. (Five Hours with Mario.) Barcelona: Ediciones Destino, 1966.

Fuentes, Carlos. *The Death of Artemio Cruz*. Translated by Sam Hileman. New York: Farrar, Straus and Giroux, 1964. Spanish original published 1962.

Gaines, Ernest J. *A Lesson before Dying*. New York: Vintage Paperback Editions, 1994.

Hardy, Thomas. *Tess of the D'Urbervilles: A Pure Woman*. Harmondsworth: Penguin English Library, 1978. First published in 1891.

Joyce, James. "The Dead." In *Dubliners: Text, Criticism, and Notes*, edited by Robert Scholes and A. Walton Litz, pp. 175–226. New York: Viking, 1969. First published in 1916.

Mann, Thomas. *Death in Venice (A Norton Critical Edition)*. Translated and edited by Clayton Koelb. New York: W. W. Norton, 1994. German original published in 1912.

———. *The Magic Mountain*. Translated by H. T. Lowe-Porter. Important Books, 2013. German original published in 1924.

Naylor, Gloria. *Mama Day*. 1988; repr., New York: Vintage Books, Random House, 1993.

O'Donohue, John. *Anam Cara: A Book of Celtic Wisdom*. New York: Harper Perennial, 1998.

————. *To Bless the Space between Us*. New York: Doubleday, 2008.

Rilke, Rainer Maria. *The Notebooks of Malte Laurids Brigge*. Translated by Michael Hulse. London and New York: Penguin, 2009. German original published in 1910.

Tolstoy, Leo. *The Death of Ivan Ilyich* and *Confession*. Translated by Peter Carson. New York and London: Liveright Publishing, a Division of W. W. Norton, 2014. Russian original of "Ivan Ilyich" published in 1886.

NOTES

CHAPTER 1: WHAT IS LIFE WITH DEATH?

1. Rainer Maria Rilke, *The Notebooks of Malte Laurids Brigge*, trans. Stephen Mitchell (New York: Random House, 1982). Originally published in 1910 as *Die Aufzeichnungen des Malte Laurids Brigge*.

2. Irene Kacandes, *Daddy's War: Greek American Stories, A Paramemoir* (2009; repr., Lincoln: University of Nebraska Press, 2012).

3. Harper Lee, *To Kill a Mockingbird* (Philadelphia: Lippincott, 1960). This was made into a movie (1962) and a play (1990).

4. See Kacandes, *Daddy's War*, pp. 6–7.

5. Sarah Palin, quoted in Ben Schott, "Death Panel," *Schott's Vocab* (*New York Times* blog), http://schott.blogs.nytimes.com/2009/08/10/death-panel/ (accessed on Feb. 23, 2012).

6. Long after Irene originally wrote these words to Steve, a friend told her about and she then read with relief *Knocking on Heaven's Door: The Path to a Better Way of Death* by Katy Butler (New York: Scribner, 2013), in which Butler considers these same issues, also in relation to a family member's pacemaker (in Butler's case, her father's).

7. Thomas Mann's *Der Zauberberg* was originally published in German in 1924. It was first translated into English by H. T. Lowe-Porter (Thomas Mann, *The Magic Mountain* [New York: Alfred A. Knopf, 1927]). The passage mentioned by Irene occurs in chapter 6, section "Snow" (New York: Vintage Books edition, 1969), pp. 469–98.

8. Rilke, *Malte Laurids Brigge*, p. 4.

9. John O'Donohue, *To Bless the Space between Us: A Book of Blessings* (New York: Doubleday, 2008). See "For a Friend on the Arrival of Illness," p. 60.

10. Ibid., pp. 61–62.

11. Steve's client who wrote these words sent them to him, understanding that they might be used in this book. He continued to see her throughout her cancer journey, including only a day or so before her long battle ended with her death in 2014.

CHAPTER 2: IS DYING AN INJUSTICE?

1. While it is still unclear what role genetics play in developing multiple sclerosis, individuals with a first-degree relative are at higher risk. See "Who Gets MS? (Epidemiology)," National Multiple Sclerosis Society, http://www.nationalmssociety.org/What-is-MS/Who-Gets-MS (accessed April 24, 2015)—among other sources—for more information about the disease.

2. David Servan-Schreiber, *On peut se dire au revoir plusieurs fois* (Paris: Robert Laffont, 2011), p. 78. Irene Kacandes's translation.

3. Ibid., pp. 78–79, Irene Kacandes's translation.

4. Martha Minow, "Surviving Victim Talk," *UCLA Law Review* 40 (1993): 1411–45.

5. Aleksandar Hemon, "The Aquarium: Personal History," *New Yorker* 87, no. 17 (June 13–June 20, 2011).

6. Ibid.

7. Elisabeth Kübler-Ross, *Living with Death and Dying* (New York: Macmillan, 1981); and Kübler-Ross, *On Children and Death* (New York: Macmillan, 1983).

8. Stephen Levine and Ondrea Levine, *Who Dies? An Investigation of Conscious Living and Conscious Dying* (New York: Anchor Books, Doubleday, 1982).

9. Ibid., p. 102.

10. Ibid., p. 103.

11. Ibid.

12. Ibid.

13. "Xolani Nkosi Johnson," *New York Times*, December 4, 2004, A19.

14. Joan Halifax, *Being with Dying* (Boston: Shambhala Publications, 2008), p. 6.

CHAPTER 3: HOW DO I HANDLE PAIN AT END OF LIFE?

1. John O'Donohue, *Anam Cara: A Book of Celtic Wisdom* (New York: Harper Perennial, 1997), p. 102.

2. Ira Byock served as director of Palliative Medicine at Dartmouth-Hitchcock Medical Center in Lebanon, New Hampshire, from 2003 through July 2013. He now serves as executive director and chief medical officer for the Institute for Human Caring, of Providence Health and Services, and continues to lecture on and advocate for better palliative and end-of-life care. See, too, irabyock.org/ (accessed April 24, 2015).

3. Joanne Lynn and Joan Harrold, *Handbook for Mortals: Guidance for People Facing Serious Illness* (New York: Oxford University Press, 1999).

4. *Halt auf freier Strecke* [Stopped on Track], directed by Andreas Dresen (2011).

5. Francis Poulenc's opera, *Dialogues des Carmélites*, was composed in 1956 and first premiered at La Scala in 1957. Poulenc based his libretto on a play by the prolific writer Georges Bernanos that was published only after Bernanos's death in 1948. Bernanos in turn had taken the material from Gertrud von Le Fort. It's difficult to find any of these written texts except in specialized libraries, but there are quite a few recordings of the opera. Irene has seen productions at the Staatsoper in Hamburg, Germany, and the Komische Oper in Berlin, Germany.

6. Michel de Montaigne, *The Essays: A Selection*, trans. M. A. Screech (Harmondsworth: Penguin, 1994), p. 24.

CHAPTER 4: WHAT ABOUT CAREGIVING?

1. Ira Byock, *Dying Well* (New York: Riverhead, 1997). Originally published with the subtitle *The Prospect for Growth at the End of Life*; reissued in 1998 with the subtitle *Peace and Possibilities at the End of Life*.

2. "Death with dignity" legislation was signed into Vermont law as "An act relating to patient choice and control at end of life" on May 20, 2013. Similar in content to the laws previously passed in Oregon and Washington, Vermont was the first state to have such a law voted in by the legislature.

3. The German film is mentioned in the previous chapter: *Halt auf freier Strecke* [Stopped on Track], directed by Andreas Dresen (2011). After this exchange between Irene and Steve took place, another European movie represented the unglamorous side of caretaking, Michael Haneke's *Amour* (2012), which won the Academy Award for Best Foreign Language Film.

4. Irene Kacandes recounts Pierre Janet's treatment of the "hysteric" Irène in an analysis of storytelling and trauma; see *Talk Fiction: Literature and the Talk Explosion* (Lincoln: University of Nebraska Press, 2001), pp. 92–94. It was a key case study for Janet himself, and he recounted it in several of his studies, including *Psychological Healing: A Historical and Clinical Study*, vol. 1, trans. Eden Paul and Cedar Paul (New York: Macmillan, 1925).

5. David Foster Wallace, *This Is Water: Some Thoughts, Delivered on a Significant Occasion, about Living a Compassionate Life* (New York: Little Brown, 2009).

NOTES

CHAPTER 5: IS SUDDEN DEATH DIFFERENT?

1. Irene Kacandes, "9/11/01=1/27/01: The Changed Posttraumatic Self," in *Trauma at Home: After 9/11*, ed. Judith Greenberg (Lincoln: University of Nebraska Press, 2003), pp. 168–83.

2. See, for instance, Susan Brison, *Aftermath: Violence and the Remaking of a Self* (Princeton: Princeton University Press, 2002), p. 40.

3. Sogyal Rinpoche, *The Tibetan Book of Living and Dying* (New York: HarperCollins, 1994), p. 7.

4. Ibid., pp. 7–8.

5. Bernard Crettaz, *vous parler de la mort* (Ayer: Porte-Plumes, 2003).

6. Yvonne Preiswerk, *Le Repas de la mort: Catholiques et protestants aux enterrements. Visages de la culture populaire en Anniviers et aux Ormonts* (Sierre, Switzerland: Monographie, 1983).

7. For an article about the exhibition written by Elisabeth Chardon and reproduced with permission from *Le Temps* (October 30, 1999), see Le culture actif suisse, http://www. culturactif. ch/livredumois/manuelvivre. htm (accessed on April 15, 2015).

8. Bernard Crettaz, *Cafés mortels: Sortir la mort du silence* (Geneva: Editions Labor et Fides, 2010).

9. For more details about Crettaz's processing of his wife's death, see "Quand meurt la femme du thanatologue," *L'Hebdo*, October 28, 1999, http://www. hebdo. ch/quand_meurt_la_femme_du_thanatologue_8109_. html (accessed April 15, 2015).

10. Irene was surprised and pleased to learn that longtime hospice nurse Barbara Karnes makes an excellent suggestion that addresses this situation. She tells helpers that when they remake the bed after the body of the deceased has been removed from it, they should place some personal object on the pillow or bedspread so that survivors who come into the room do not experience the event of the death quite as brutally as Irene did when she saw the empty bed Takis had lain in. See Barbara Karnes, *The Final Act of Living: Reflections of a Longtime Hospice Nurse*, rev. ed. (2003; repr., Vancouver, WA: Barbara Karnes Books, 2012), pp. 132–33. Irene had bumped into Karnes's name somewhere during this journey with Steve, but she did not manage to track down her work and read it until almost the end of preparing the manuscript for publication. In clear, direct language, Karnes does a marvelous job of laying out topics like living with a life-threatening illness, signs of dying, the grieving process, and so on, in *The Final Act* which covers most of these subjects, and in a series of very short booklets and even DVDs that focus on one topic. For more on Barbara Karnes and the materials she has available, see her website, www.bkbooks.com (accessed April 15, 2015).

CHAPTER 6: WHAT COMES AFTER I DIE?

1. Thomas Lynch, *Bodies in Motion and at Rest: On Metaphor and Mortality, Essays* (New York: Norton, 2000).

2. Ibid., pp. 90–91.

3. Alexander Schmemann, *O Death, Where Is Thy Sting?* trans. Alexis Vinogradov (Crestwood, NY: St. Vladimir's Seminary, 2003).

4. For more information about the exhibition, see "Noch Mal Leben," www.noch-mal-leben.de (accessed April 14, 2015). For the book, consult Beate Lakotta and Walter Schels, *Noch mal leben vor dem Tod. Wenn Menschen sterben* (Munich: Deutsch Verlags-Anstalt, 2004).

5. *Valley News*, Saturday, December 16, 2006. Also, "Body Worlds: The Original Exhibition of Real Human Bodies," www.bodyworlds.com (accessed April 24, 2015).

6. See "Rainer Maria Rilke's 'Requiem for a Friend,' as Translated from the German by Stephen Mitchell," http://www.paratheatrical.com/requiemtext.html (accessed February 21, 2015). The original German text can be found in a number of sources, including, Rainer Maria Rilke, "Für eine Freundin," in *Werke in drei Bänden, Band 1. Gedicht-Zyklen* (Munich: Insel Verlag, 1955), pp. 401–12.

7. Louise Erdrich, *The Last Report on the Miracles at Little No Horse* (New York: HarperCollins, 2001).

8. The novel did indeed appear later that year. See Louise Erdrich, *The Round House* (New York: Harper, 2012).

9. Jessica Mitford, *The American Way of Death* (New York: Simon and Schuster, 1963), and *The American Way of Death Revisited* (New York: Alfred A. Knopf, 1998).

10. Simone de Beauvoir, *Une Mort très douce. Récit* (Paris: Gallimard, 1964). The book appeared in English as *A Very Easy Death*, trans. Patrick O'Brian (1965; repr., New York: Putnam, 1966).

11. Ibid., p. 150, in original French edition; Irene's translation.

12. Benjamin Noys, *The Culture of Death* (Oxford and New York: Berg, 2005).

13. "A Definition of Irreversible Coma: Report of the Ad Hoc Committee of the Harvard Medical School to Examine the Definition of Brain Death," *JAMA* 205 (1968): 337–40.

14. J. Mark Barna and Elizabeth J. Barna, *A Christian Ending: A Handbook for Burial in the Ancient Christian Tradition* (Manton, CA: Divine Ascent, 2011).

15. There are many sources of additional information, but one great news story you can listen to from National Public Radio is "Green Burial Movement Spreads to the

Southwest," http://www.npr.org/templates/story/story.php?storyId=6119301 (accessed April 14, 2015). See, too, the websites of Green Burial Council and Green Burials, at greenburialcouncil.org and greenburials.org, respectively (accessed April 14, 2015).

16. Lynch, *Bodies in Motion and at Rest*, p. 126.

17. Mary Roach, *Stiff: The Curious Lives of Human Cadavers* (New York: W. W. Norton, 2003).

18. Several years after Irene and Steve had this exchange, Irene learned more about Vesalius from *Body of Work: Meditations on Mortality from the Human Anatomy Lab* by Christine Montross (New York: Penguin, 2007). Montross's book reproduces many of Vesalius's images. Hers is a highly original memoir that recounts the author's anatomy course during her first semester of medical school, provides information on the history of dissection—including Vesalius's role—and contemplates aging and death.

19. Emmanuelle Huisman-Perrin, *La Mort expliquée à ma fille* (Paris: Seuil, 2002).

20. Written by "Eugène" and illustrated by "Bertola," *La Mort à vivre* (Geneva: Editions La Joie de Lire, 1999).

21. Paul Vitello, "Revising a Ritual of Tending to the Dead," *New York Times*, December 13, 2010, A17 (New York edition), http://www.nytimes.com/2010/12/13/nyregion/13burial.html?pagewanted=all&_r=0 (accessed April 10, 2015).

22. Father Luke A. Veronis, comp. and ed., *Lynette's Hope: The Witness of Lynette Katherine Hoppe's Life and Death* (Ben Lomond, CA: Conciliar Press Ministries, 2008).

23. See, for instance, Fr. Patrick Henry Reardon, "The Death of Lynette Hoppe, Missionary to Albania," http://www.orthodoxytoday.org/articles6/ReardonHoppeAlbania.php (accessed April 10, 2015).

24. David Servan-Schreiber, *On peut se dire au revoir plusieurs fois* (Paris: Robert Laffont, 2011), translated as *Not the Last Good-bye: On Life, Death, Healing and Cancer* (New York: Viking, 2011).

25. Don Piper with Cecil Murphey, *90 Minutes in Heaven: A True Story of Death and Life* (Grand Rapids, MI: Revell, 2004); for the young readers' version, see Don Piper with Cecil Murphey, *90 Minutes in Heaven: My True Story (A Special Edition for Young Readers)* (Grand Rapids, MI: Revell, 2009).

26. Megory Anderson, *Sacred Dying: Creating Rituals for Embracing the End of Life* (2001; repr., New York: Marlowe, 2003).

CHAPTER 7: WHAT ABOUT GRIEF?

1. Sogyal Rinpoche, *The Tibetan Book of Living and Dying* (New York: HarperCollins, 1994), p. 311.

2. Ibid., p. 316.

3. For those unfamiliar with these terms and practices, there are many sources of information. One we find helpful is Lori Palatnik, "ABCs of Death & Mourning: Coping with the Emotional and Spiritual Issues of This Difficult Time," Aish.com, aish.com/jl/l/dam/ABCs_of_Death__Mourning.html (accessed April 12, 2015). See also the references in note 4.

4. There are many, many books, manuals, and websites that talk about these traditions. One fairly comprehensive book is Maurice Lamm's *The Jewish Way in Death and Mourning* (Middle Village, NY: Jonathan David Publishers, 2000). A clear explanation of standing up after sitting shiva can be found at Zalman Goldstein, "The Last Day of Shiva," Chabad.org, http://www.chabad.org/library/article_cdo/aid/371151/jewish/The-Last-Day-of-Shiva.htm (accessed March 16, 2015).

5. There are many editions of this novel that was first published in 1891. This quote is taken from Thomas Hardy, *Tess of the D'Urbervilles: A Pure Woman* (Harmondsworth, England: Penguin, 1978), pp. 149–50.

6. Ibid., p. 150.

7. Originally drafted in 1907 but not published in *Dubliners* until 1916, "The Dead" can be found today in many editions and anthologies. One helpful edition is James Joyce, *Dubliners: Text, Criticism, and Notes*, ed. Robert Scholes and A. Walton Litz (New York: Viking, 1969), pp. 175–226.

8. Irving Townsend, *Separate Lifetimes* (Exeter, NH: J. N. Townsend Publishing, 1986), p. 172.

9. Joanne Lynn and Joan Harrold, *Handbook for Mortals: Guidance for People Facing Serious Illness* (New York: Oxford University Press, 1999); see esp. pp. 71–84.

10. Stephen Levine and Ondrea Levine, *Who Dies? An Investigation of Conscious Living and Conscious Dying* (1982; repr., New York: Anchor Books, 1989), p. 115.

11. Ira Byock, *Dying Well: Peace and Possibilities at the End of Life* (New York: Riverhead, 1998); Byock, *The Four Things That Matter Most: A Book about Living* (New York: Free Press, 2004); Byock, *The Best Care Possible: A Physician's Quest to Transform Care through the End of Life* (New York: Avery/Penguin, 2012).

CHAPTER 8: WHAT'S SO GREAT ABOUT MORTALITY ANYWAY?

1. John O'Donohue, "Beannacht," *Anam Cara: A Book of Celtic Wisdom* (New York: Harper Perennial, 1997), unnumbered.

2. Stephen Cave, *Immortality: The Quest to Live Forever and How It Drives Civilization* (New York: Crown, 2012).

3. Rainer Maria Rilke, *The Notebooks of Malte Laurids Brigge*, trans. Stephen Mitchell (New York: Random House, 1982), p. 4. Originally published in 1910 as *Die Aufzeichnungen des Malte Laurids Brigge*.

4. For more on Lee Webster, New Hampshire Funeral Resources, Education, and Advocacy, and the argument for a "green" or "natural" burial, see "NH Funeral Resources, Education & Advocacy," www.nhfuneral.org (accessed April 13, 2015). In the last stages of editing this book, we learned about a new movement to compost human remains. This would be the most ecological method of all, but the authors of this book are still trying to wrap their minds around that one! See Catrin Einhorn, "Returning the Dead to Nature: Some Environmental Advocates Say Bodies Should Be Composted, Not Buried," *New York Times*, Sciences Times, Tuesday April 14, 2015, D1, D5.

5. Bernard Crettaz's Cafés mortels were the first type of open discussions of death Irene and Steve encountered, and that was through Crettaz himself in Switzerland. Since that time, however, the idea of talking with friends or even strangers about death has taken on many forms in many places, including in the United States, where Death Cafe (deathcafe.com) boasted about more than 2,144 meetings (accessed July 21, 2015). The similar Death Salon (deathsalon.org) is having comparable success in setting up discussions across America, but appears to want to exercise tight control over use of that name (accessed July 21, 2015). To cite one more example, Death over Dinner (deathoverdinner. org) launched a special drive for a barrage of meetings to be held during the first week of January 2014 (accessed July 8, 2014). We even read about a "death rehearsal" sponsored by two therapists in Oakland, California, in 2009 (Becky Palmstrom, "Rehearsing Your Own Death: Not Your Typical Night in Oakland," *Oakland North*, December 1, 2009 http://oaklandnorth.net/2009/12/01/rehearsing-your-own-death-not-your-typical-night-in-oakland/ [accessed July 8, 2014]).

6. O'Donohue, *Anam Cara*, p. 202.

7. Stephen and Ondrea Levine, *Who Dies? An Investigation of Conscious Living and Conscious Dying* (1982; repr., New York: Anchor Books, 1989), p. 163 et passim.

8. David Servan-Schreiber, *On peut se dire au revoir plusieurs fois* (Paris: Robert

Laffont, 2011), translated as *Not the Last Good-bye: On Life, Death, Healing and Cancer* (New York: Viking, 2011).

AFTERWORD

1. Anton Grosz, *How Do I Live When I Know I'm Going to Die? Thoughts and Insights about Life's Most Challenging Passage and America's Last Taboo: Including Information on Hospice Care at End-of-Life* (San Francisco: FMA Books, 2001). Irene was greatly comforted by the view of longtime hospice nurse Barbara Karnes, who believes: "There is really no such action as dying. . . . We are either alive or dead. The space in between is called living." In *The Final Act of Living: Reflections of a Longtime Hospice Nurse* (2003; repr., Vancouver, WA: Barbara Karnes Books, [rev.] 2012), p. 34.

INDEX

306.9   Gordon, Steve,
G   1956-

             Let's talk about
             death.

DATE		

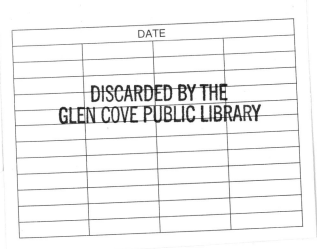